Guide

To Nonprofit Development

By

Dan Moore, Sr.

ISBN-10: 1475208774
ISBN-13: 978-1475208771

Edited By Jasmine Saxon

This guide is designed to share information about nonprofit development. It is not a legal or financial document and is not intended to replace advice from an attorney, accountant or competent professional. It is recommended that you seek professional advice to answer any questions or concerns.

Let your light so shine before men that they may see your good works,

and glorify your Father which is in heaven.

Matthew 5:16

INTRODUCTION

Before you take that step to form a nonprofit organization there are a number of questions you need to ask.

1. Why are you starting this nonprofit?
2. What are your qualifications?
3. What are your strengths and weaknesses?
4. Who is the audience you will serve?
5. Are you presently engaged in this work and if so, how long?
6. What are your expectations for this nonprofit?
7. Do you have help in forming this organization?

While this guide is published to help and offer information, it is not intended to give legal or accounting advice or to replace counsel from competent professionals. This guide is based on starting a nonprofit in Georgia and laws or requirements may vary in other states.

It is recommended that you assess your motivation and research to see if there are others providing a similar service or product. You may want to seek out other organizations and meet with someone there regarding the pros and cons of their organization and the challenges and successes they have experienced.

If after this exercise you are sure you want to proceed and are confident it can succeed then begin this simple step-by-step guide. Here's hoping that you will provide services to those in need and be fulfilled in helping others.

One of the first steps is to incorporate. Georgia makes this step very easy and you can file this application online. Do a name search to make sure the name you have selected is available in your state. In Georgia visit the website of the Georgia Secretary of State. www.sos.ga.gov Click on "Corporate Search" and go to Search for a Business Entity. If the name is available you may wish to reserve it but this is not necessary if you are ready to file online.

You will need the following:

A new domestic Corporation (Profit, Non-profit, Professional Corporation, Professional Association)

- Name of the corporation or a valid Name Reservation Number
- Name and address of the person filing for the corporation
- A valid email address
- Mailing Address of the Principal Office
- Name and Address of the Registered Agent (must be a physical street address in Georgia where an individual can be located in-person for the company)
- Name and address of *each* incorporator

- # of Authorized shares (This step does NOT apply to nonprofits)
- Any optional provisions you need to add to your Articles of Incorporation *
- A valid major Credit Card including the 3-digit security code from the signature panel on back and the expiration date (we accept MC, VISA, AMEX and Discover Cards) or a valid ACH account.

*If you intend to apply for a 501(c)(3) exemption it is imperative that you add the following optional provisions to comply with the requirements of the IRS.

Article 6 (or appropriate #)

None of the net earnings of the corporation shall inure to the benefit of, or be distributable to its members, trustees, officers or other private persons, except that the corporation shall be authorized and empowered to pay reasonable compensation for services rendered and to make payments and distributions in furtherance of the purposes set forth in Article 2 hereof. No substantial part of the activities of the corporation shall be the carrying on of propaganda, or otherwise attempting to influence legislation, and the corporation shall not participate in, or intervene in (including the publishing or distribution of statements) any political campaign on behalf of or in opposition to any candidate for public office. Notwithstanding any other provision of these articles, this corporation shall not, except to an unsubstantial degree, engage in any activity or exercise any powers that are not in furtherance of the purpose of this corporation.

Article 7 (or appropriate #)

Upon dissolution of the corporation, assets shall be distributed for one or more exempt purposes within the meaning of section 501 (c) (3) of the Internal revenue Code, or the corresponding section of any future federal tax code, or shall be distributed to the federal government, or to a state or local government, for a public purpose. Any such assets not so disposed of shall be disposed of by a Court of Competent Jurisdiction of the county in which the principal office is then located, exclusively for such purposes or to such organizations. As said Court shall determine, which are organized and operated exclusively for such purposes.

This is a SAMPLE of filing to incorporate in Georgia.

Articles of Incorporation
Of
Your organization name, Inc.

Article 1.

The name of the corporation is ***your organization name***, Inc.

Article 2.

The corporation is organized pursuant to the Georgia Nonprofit Code. It is organized exclusively for charitable, religious, educational, and scientific purposes, including, for such purposes, the making of distributions to organizations that qualify as exempt organizations under section 501 (c)(3) of the Internal Revenue Code, or the corresponding section of any future federal tax code.

Article 3.

The street address of the registered office is (Street address-no post office box)
The registered agent at such address is (name of registered agent) The County of the registered office is _____

Article 4.

The name and address of each incorporator, all of whom are citizens of the United States, is: (Provide name and address of each incorporator – May only require one person. Verify with state requirements)

Article 5.

The corporation will not have members.

Article 6.

None of the net earnings of the corporation shall inure to the benefit of, or be distributable to its members, trustees, officers or other private persons, except that the corporation shall be authorized and empowered to pay reasonable compensation for services rendered and to make payments and distributions in furtherance of the purposes set forth in Article 2 hereof. No substantial part of the activities of the corporation shall be the carrying on of propaganda, or otherwise attempting to influence legislation, and the corporation shall not participate in, or intervene in (including the publishing or distribution of statements) any political campaign on behalf of or in opposition to any candidate for public office. Notwithstanding any other provision of these articles, this corporation shall not, except to an unsubstantial degree, engage in any activity or exercise any powers that are not in furtherance of the purpose of this corporation.

Article 7.

Upon dissolution of the corporation, assets shall be distributed for one or more exempt purposes within the meaning of section 501 (c) (3) of the Internal revenue Code, or the corresponding section of any future federal tax code, or shall be distributed to the federal government, or to a state or local government, for a public purpose. Any such assets not so disposed of shall be disposed of by a Court of Competent Jurisdiction of the county in which the principal office is then located, exclusively for such purposes or to such organizations. As said Court shall determine, which are organized and operated exclusively for such purposes.

Article 8.

The principal mailing address of the corporation is (mailing address here)

IN WITNESS WHEREOF, the undersigned has executed these Articles of Incorporation
This   day of   ,

_____
(Name of Incorporator)

Name of your County Legal Newspaper in Georgia. (This can be found online by placing in your county and its legal organ)

Dear Publisher:

Notice is given that the articles of incorporation that will incorporate **Your Company Name** have been delivered to the secretary of state for filing in accordance with the Georgia Nonprofit Corporation Code. The initial registered office of the corporation is located at **Your Address, City, State, and Zip** and its initial registered agent at such address is **your name.**

Enclosed is a check in the amount of $40.00 in payment of the cost of publishing this notice.

Sincerely,

Your Name

Next, you will need an Employer Identification Number EIN. This is form SS-4 and can be filed online at www.IRS.gov/businesses or

Apply By EIN Toll-Free Telephone Service

Taxpayers can obtain an EIN immediately by calling the Business & Specialty Tax Line at (800) 829-4933. The hours of operation are 7:00 a.m. - 10:00 p.m. local time, Monday through Friday. An assistor takes the information, assigns the EIN, and provides the number to an authorized individual over the telephone.

Form **SS-4**	**Application for Employer Identification Number**	OMB No. 1545-0003
(Rev. January 2010)	(For use by employers, corporations, partnerships, trusts, estates, churches, government agencies, Indian tribal entities, certain individuals, and others.)	EIN
Department of the Treasury Internal Revenue Service	▶ See separate instructions for each line. ▶ Keep a copy for your records.	

Type or print clearly.

1 Legal name of entity (or individual) for whom the EIN is being requested
My Nonprofit, Inc.

2 Trade name of business (if different from name on line 1)

3 Executor, administrator, trustee, "care of" name
Mr. Servant

4a Mailing address (room, apt., suite no. and street, or P.O. box)
123Need Street

5a Street address (if different) (Do not enter a P.O. box.)

4b City, state, and ZIP code (if foreign, see instructions)
My Town, IM 00000

5b City, state, and ZIP code (if foreign, see instructions)

6 County and state where principal business is located
Samaria

7a Name of responsible party
Mr. Servant

7b SSN, ITIN, or EIN
123-45-678

8a Is this application for a limited liability company (LLC) (or a foreign equivalent)?   ☐ Yes ☑ No

8b If 8a is "Yes," enter the number of LLC members ▶

8c If 8a is "Yes," was the LLC organized in the United States?   ☐ Yes ☐ No

9a Type of entity (check only one box) Caution. If 8a is "Yes," see the instructions for the correct box to check.

☐ Sole proprietor (SSN)
☐ Partnership
☑ Corporation (enter form number to be filed) ▶
☐ Personal service corporation
☐ Church or church-controlled organization
☐ Other nonprofit organization (specify) ▶
☐ Other (specify) ▶

☐ Estate (SSN of decedent)
☐ Plan administrator (TIN)
☐ Trust (TIN of grantor)
☐ National Guard   ☐ State/local government
☐ Farmers' cooperative   ☐ Federal government/military
☐ REMIC   ☐ Indian tribal governments/enterprises
Group Exemption Number (GEN) if any ▶

9b If a corporation, name the state or foreign country (if applicable) where incorporated
State: Home State   Foreign country:

10 Reason for applying (check only one box)

☑ Started new business (specify type) ▶
☐ Hired employees (Check the box and see line 13.)
☐ Compliance with IRS withholding regulations
☐ Other (specify) ▶

☐ Banking purpose (specify purpose) ▶
☐ Changed type of organization (specify new type) ▶
☐ Purchased going business
☐ Created a trust (specify type) ▶
☐ Created a pension plan (specify type) ▶

11 Date business started or acquired (month, day, year). See instructions.
01/01/2016

12 Closing month of accounting year

13 Highest number of employees expected in the next 12 months (enter -0- if none).
If no employees expected, skip line 14.

Agricultural	Household	Other
0	0	0

14 If you expect your employment tax liability to be $1,000 or less in a full calendar year and want to file Form 944 annually instead of Forms 941 quarterly, check here. (Your employment tax liability generally will be $1,000 or less if you expect to pay $4,000 or less in total wages.) If you do not check this box, you must file Form 941 for every quarter. ☐

15 First date wages or annuities were paid (month, day, year). Note. If applicant is a withholding agent, enter date income will first be paid to nonresident alien (month, day, year) ▶

16 Check one box that best describes the principal activity of your business.
☐ Construction   ☐ Rental & leasing   ☐ Transportation & warehousing
☐ Real estate   ☐ Manufacturing   ☐ Finance & insurance
☐ Health care & social assistance   ☐ Wholesale agent/broker
☐ Accommodation & food service   ☐ Wholesale other   ☐ Retail
☑ Other (specify) non-profit

17 Indicate principal line of merchandise sold, specific construction work done, products produced, or services provided
NA

18 Has the applicant entity shown on line 1 ever applied for and received an EIN? ☐ Yes ☑ No
If "Yes," write previous EIN here ▶

Third Party Designee
Complete this section only if you want to authorize the named individual to receive the entity's EIN and answer questions about the completion of this form.

Designee's name:
Designee's telephone number (include area code) ( )
Address and ZIP code:
Designee's fax number (include area code) ( )

Under penalties of perjury, I declare that I have examined this application, and to the best of my knowledge and belief, it is true, correct, and complete.

Name and title (type or print clearly) ▶ Mr. Servant, President
Applicant's telephone number (include area code) (123) 456-789

Signature ▶   Date ▶
Applicant's fax number (include area code) ( )

For Privacy Act and Paperwork Reduction Act Notice, see separate instructions.   Cat. No. 16055N   Form **SS-4** (Rev. 1-2010)

If you intend to seek grants from individuals and corporations most will require your organization to have a 501 (c) (3) status. This allows contributors to take a tax exemption on all or a portion of their donation depending on its purpose. (Seek appropiate counsel for clarification)

Note: while a 501 (c) (3) is required by most funders, keep in mind it is not a guarentee of funding. This (5) (0) (1) (c) (3) number is not a winning lottery number. It is simply the first step in qualifying for grants.

The application is filed on form 1023 available from the IRS website. To cmplete the application there are several things you will need.

1. By-Laws
2. Conflict of Interest policy
3. EIN number
4. 3 year budget projects

If you do not have legal or accounting advice, which is recommended, you can find By-Laws on line that you can modify as needed. The same is with a conflict of interest policy. Sample copies are provided here for your convenience.

Bylaws
of
(Your Organization name)

Article I.

Name and Purpose

1. The name of this corporation shall be **(Your Organization name)**

2. The principle offices of this corporation shall be located in _____ County, Georgia.
3. The purpose and mission of this corporation is
_____
4. This corporation is organized exclusively for charitable and educational purposes, including, for such purposes, the making of distributions to organizations that qualify as exempt under Section 501(c)(3) of the Internal Revenue Code, or the corresponding Section of any future Federal Tax Code.
5. This corporation provides equal opportunities in employment and programming, including Title IX and ADA requirements.

Article II

Members
1. This corporation shall have no members.

Article III

Board of Directors

1. **General:** Responsibility for day-to-day management of the nonprofit corporation shall be vested in a Board of Directors, which shall consist of no fewer than three (3) and no more than seventeen (17) members. All members of the Board have equal voting rights and privileges.
2. **Qualifications:** A Director shall be committed to the purpose and rules of this corporation.
3. **Terms:** Initially directors shall be elected to serve staggered terms of office of one (1), two (2), and three (3) years. After the setting of staggered terms, a Director shall serve for a term of two years. A Director may serve for two or more consecutive terms. Elections shall be held at the annual meeting. Each director shall serve until his or her successor has been elected and qualified.
4. **Vacancies:** Vacancies on the Board shall be filled by a vote of the majority of the Corporation's Directors.
5. **Resignation:** Any Director may resign at any time by giving written notice to the President or to the Secretary. The resignation of any Director shall take effect at the time specified in such notice, and, unless otherwise specified therein, the acceptance of such resignation shall not be necessary to make it effective.
6. **Compensation:** Directors shall not be paid compensation for the performance of their duties.
7. **Removal:** The position of a Director with three unexcused absences from consecutive regular meetings shall be immediately vacant.

Article IV

Officers

1. **Officers:** Officers of this corporation shall be a Chief Executive Officer, Vice-President, Secretary, and Treasurer, all of whom must be Directors.
2. **Terms:** The officers shall be elected for terms of two years by a majority vote of the Board of Directors. Officers may succeed themselves. All officers shall hold office until their successors have been duly elected and qualified.
3. **Responsibilities:**
   a. The Chief Executive Officer (CEO) (or, in his/ her absence, the Vice President) shall preside at all meetings of the Board of Directors; shall present a report annually of the work of the Corporation for the preceding year at the annual meeting; shall appoint all committees with the consent of the majority of the Board of Directors; and shall be an ex officio member of all committees

   b. The Vice President shall assist the CEO in carrying out his/her activities, and shall act on behalf of the CEO in his/her absence.
   c. The Secretary shall issue notice of all meetings; shall be responsible for the keeping and maintaining of corporate minutes, records, reports, and other documents pertaining to the affairs of the Corporation.

d. The Treasurer shall be responsible for the custody of all moneys and securities of the Corporation, and shall have responsibility for the keeping of regular books of account with respect thereto.

4. **Vacancies:** Vacancies in any of the offices of the Corporation shall be filled for the unexpired term by a majority vote of the Board.

5. **Resignation.** Any officer may resign at any time by giving written notice to the CEO or to the Secretary. The resignation of any officer shall take effect at the time specified in such notice, and, unless otherwise specified therein, the acceptance of such resignation shall not be necessary to make it effective.

Article V.

Meetings and Committees

1. **Annual Meetings:** The annual meeting of the Board shall be held each year, at a time and place convenient to members of the Board. The Board of Directors shall establish the date, time, and place of each meeting. The Secretary shall give adequate notice to the members of the board of not less than (5) five and no more than (33) thirty-three days before the meeting date.

2. **Special Meetings:** Special meetings of the Board may be called at any time by the CEO, or by a majority of the members of the Board. The Secretary shall give adequate notice to all members of the Board, not less than three days before the special meeting. The notice calling for a special meeting of the Board shall state the purpose(s) thereof.

3. **Consent and Waiver.** The timeline provision for notice of the preceding sections need not apply if consent and waiver forms are signed by a majority of the Directors.

4. **Quorum:** Members present at a properly noticed meeting shall constitute a quorum to do business.

5. **Unanimous written consent:** A decision of the Board shall be valid and official without a meeting of the Board, if the decision in writing is signed by all members of the Board.

6. **Standing Committees:** The Board shall maintain three standing committees:
   a. **Finance.** The Treasurer is Chairperson of the Finance Committee. The Finance Committee shall be charged with developing the annual budget and reviewing the books and accounts.
   b. **Public Relations Committee:** The Public Relations Committee shall be charged with development of any advertising materials, recruitment, fund-raising, and any publicity efforts.
   c. **Program Committee:** The Program committee shall be charged with the general oversight of program planning and review.

7. **Proxy Votes:** A proxy vote in writing shall be considered valid for actions requiring a majority of the Directors and will be held for a period not less than twelve (12) months.

Article VI.

Finances

All financial accounts in any financial institution shall be held in the name of the Corporation with authority in either the CEO or an officer of the Corporation, or an Individual authorized by a majority vote of the Board to act and sign for the Corporation on financial matters.

Article VII.

Amendments

1. Amending Articles: The articles of incorporation may be amended by a vote of a majority of the Board of Directors.

2. Amending the Bylaws: The bylaws of this Corporation may be amended by a vote of a majority of the Board of Directors.

The bylaws were accepted on _____

Sample Copy of Conflict of Interest Policy

Your Organization, Inc.

Conflict of Interest Policy

For Officers, Directors and Staff Members

No member of Your Organization, Inc. Board of Directors or Staff shall derive any personal profit or gain, directly or indirectly, by reason of his or her participation in **Your Organization**, Inc. Each individual shall disclose to **Your Organization**, Inc. any personal interest, which he or she may have in any matter pending before the organization and shall refrain from participation in any decision on such matter. Any member of Your Organization's Board of Directors or Staff shall refrain from obtaining any list of **Your Organization**; Inc's contacts for personal or private solicitation purposes at any time during the term of their affiliation.

In addition to my service for **Your Organization**, Inc., at this time I am a Board member or an employee of the following organizations:

1.

2.

3.

This is to certify that I, except with regard to carrying out my duties as an officer, director or staff member of **Your Organization**, Inc., or as described below, am not now nor at any time during the past year have been:

1) A participant, directly or indirectly, in any arrangement, agreement, investment, or other activity with any vendor, supplier, or other party; doing business with the **Your Organization**, Inc. which has resulted or could result in person benefit to me.
2) A recipient, directly or indirectly, of any salary payments or loans or gifts of any kind or any free service or discounts or other fees from or on behalf of any person or organization engaged in any transaction with **Your Organization**, Inc.

Any exceptions to 1 or 2 above are stated below with a full description of the transactions and of the interest, whether direct or indirect, which I have (or have had during the past year) in the persons or organizations having transactions with **Your Organization**, Inc.

Signature: _____ Date _____

Printed name: _____

When it comes to filing the application many people feel intimated just looking at the number of pages in the application. First, many of the pages will not necessarily apply to your organization. There are categories that only pertain to churches, hospitals, foundations, etc.

Again, here you can choose to obtain the services of a professional or you may decide to go for it on your own. What we are providing here is a sample for guidance if you decide to file. It is not intended to provide legal or accounting service or to replace services of other professionals.

The application is form 1023 and can be downloaded from www.IRS.gov you can fill in the form and save it to go back and finish at a later date. If it is unfamiliar to you consult a professional, attend a class or workshop or solicit other assistance to make sure you are in compliance with the regulations.

There may be volunteer services in your area you can check with or organizations that may offer free or discounted services. The following sample is for reference and is intended to be a guide only.

Good News!

The IRS has changed the requirements for filing for 501 (c) (3) status. If you qualify you can file the new 1023 EZ. It is much easier and usually has a faster response time for approval. We have included information of this form but have also left the 1023 form sample here also in case you need to file this form. We will begin with the 1023 EZ.

Form 1023-EZ Eligibility Worksheet
(Must be completed prior to completing Form 1023-EZ)

If you answer "Yes" to any of the worksheet questions, you are not eligible to apply for exemption under section 501(c)(3) using Form 1023-EZ. You must apply on Form 1023. If you answer "No" to all of the worksheet questions, you may apply using Form 1023-EZ.

1.	**Do you project that your annual gross receipts will exceed $50,000 in any of the next 3 years?** Gross receipts are the total amounts the organization received from all sources during its annual accounting period, without subtracting any costs or expenses. You should consider this year and the next two years.	☐ Yes	☒ No
2.	**Have your annual gross receipts exceeded $50,000 in any of the past 3 years?**	☐ Yes	☒ No
3.	**Do you have total assets in excess of $250,000?** Total assets includes cash, accounts receivable, inventories, bonds and notes receivable, corporate stocks, loans receivable, other investments, depreciable and depletable assets, land, buildings, equipment, and any other assets.	☐ Yes	☒ No
4.	**Were you formed under the laws of a foreign country (United States territories and possessions are not considered foreign countries)?** You are formed under the laws of a foreign country if you are not formed under the laws of (1) the United States, its states, territories, or possessions; (2) federally recognized Indian tribal or Alaskan native governments; or (3) the District of Columbia.	☐ Yes	☒ No
5.	**Is your mailing address in a foreign country (United States territories and possessions are not considered foreign countries)?** Your mailing address is the address where all correspondence will be sent.	☐ Yes	☒ No
6.	**Are you a successor to, or controlled by, an entity suspended under section 501(p) (suspension of tax-exempt status of terrorist organizations)?** Section 501(p)(1) suspends the exemption from tax under section 501(a) of any organization described in section 501(p)(2). An organization is described in section 501(p)(2) if the organization is designated or otherwise individually identified (1) under certain provisions of the Immigration and Nationality Act as a terrorist organization or foreign terrorist organization; (2) in or pursuant to an Executive Order which is related to terrorism and issued under the authority of the International Emergency Economic Powers Act or section 5 of the United Nations Participation Act of 1945 for the purpose of imposing on such organization an economic or other sanction; or (3) in or pursuant to an Executive Order issued under the authority of any federal law, if the organization is designated or otherwise individually identified in or pursuant to the Executive Order as supporting or engaging in terrorist activity (as defined in the Immigration and Nationality Act) or supporting terrorism (as defined in the Foreign Relations Authorization Act) and the Executive Order refers to section 501(p)(2). Under section 501(p)(3) of the Code, suspension of an organization's tax exemption begins on the date of the first publication of a designation or identification with respect to the organization, as described above, or the date on which section 501(p) was enacted, whichever is later. This suspension continues until all designations and identifications of the organization are rescinded under the law or Executive Order under which such designation or identification was made.	☐ Yes	☒ No

7.	**Are you a limited liability company (LLC)?**	☐ Yes	☒ No
	Answer "Yes" if you are organized as an LLC under the laws of the state in which you were formed.		
8.	**Are you a successor to a for-profit entity?**	☐ Yes	☒ No
	You are a successor if you have: 1. Substantially taken over all of the assets or activities of a for-profit entity; 2. Been converted or merged from a for-profit entity; or 3. Installed the same officers, directors, or trustees as a for-profit entity that no longer exists.		
9.	**Were you previously revoked or are you a successor to a previously revoked organization (other than an organization the tax-exempt status of which was automatically revoked for failure to file a Form 990-series return for three consecutive years)?**	☐ Yes	☒ No
	Do not check "Yes" if your previous revocation, or your predecessor's revocation, was an automatic revocation (pursuant to section 6033(j)) for failing to satisfy Form 990-series filing requirements for three consecutive years.		
10.	**Are you a church or a convention or association of churches described in section 170(b)(1)(A)(i)?**	☐ Yes	☒ No
	There is no single definition of the word "church" for tax purposes; however, the characteristics generally attributed to churches include: • A distinct legal existence, • A recognized creed and form of worship, • A definite and distinct ecclesiastical government, • A formal code of doctrine and discipline, • A distinct religious history, • A membership not associated with any other church or denomination, • Ordained ministers ministering to the congregation, • Ordained ministers selected after completing prescribed courses of study, • A literature of its own, • Established places of worship, • Regular congregations, • Regular religious services, • Sunday schools for the religious instruction of the young, and • Schools for the preparation of ministers. Although it is not necessary that each of the above characteristics be present, a congregation or other religious membership group that meets regularly for religious worship is generally required. A church includes mosques, temples, synagogues, and other forms of religious organizations. For more information, see Publication 1828.		

-12-   Form 1023-EZ Instructions

14

11.	Are you a school, college, or university described in section 170(b)(1)(A)(ii)?	☐ Yes	☒ No
	An organization is a school if it: 1. Presents formal instruction as its primary function, 2. Has a regularly scheduled curriculum, 3. Has a regular faculty of qualified teachers, 4. Has a regularly enrolled student body, and 5. Has a place where educational activities are regularly carried on. The term "school" includes primary, secondary, preparatory, high schools, colleges, and universities. It does not include organizations engaged in both educational and non-educational activities, unless the latter are merely incidental to the educational activities.		
12.	Are you a hospital or medical research organization described in section 170(b)(1)(A)(iii) or a hospital organization described in section 501(r)(2)(A)(i)?	☐ Yes	☒ No
	An organization is a hospital described in section 170(b)(1)(A)(iii) if its principal purpose or function is providing medical or hospital care, or medical education or research. Medical care includes treatment of any physical or mental disability or condition, on an inpatient or outpatient basis. Thus, if an organization is a rehabilitation institution, outpatient clinic, or community mental health or drug treatment center, it is a hospital if its principal function is providing treatment services as described above. A hospital does not include convalescent homes, homes for children or the aged, or institutions whose principal purpose or function is to train handicapped individuals to pursue a vocation. An organization is a medical research organization described in section 170(b)(1)(A)(iii) if its principal purpose or function is the direct, continuous, and active conduct of medical research in conjunction with a hospital. The hospital with which the organization is affiliated must be described in section 501(c)(3), a federal hospital, or an instrumentality of a governmental unit, such as a municipal hospital. An organization is a hospital organization described in section 501(r)(2)(A)(i) if the organization operates a facility which is required by a state to be licensed, registered, or similarly recognized as a hospital.		

13.	**Are you applying for exemption as a cooperative hospital service organization under section 501(e)?**	☐Yes	☒No

A cooperative hospital service organization described in section 501(e) is organized and operated on a cooperative basis to provide its section 501(c)(3) hospital members one or more of the following activities.

- Data processing.
- Purchasing (including purchasing insurance on a group basis).
- Warehousing.
- Billing and collection (including purchasing patron accounts receivable on a recourse basis).
- Food.
- Clinical.
- Industrial engineering.
- Laboratory.
- Printing.
- Communications.
- Record center.
- Personnel (including selecting, testing, training, and educating personnel) services.

A cooperative hospital service organization must also meet certain other requirements specified in section 501(e).

14.	**Are you applying for exemption as a cooperative service organization of operating educational organizations under section 501(f)?**	☐Yes	☒No

An organization is a cooperative service organization of operating educational organizations if it is organized and operated solely to provide investment services to its members. Those members must be organizations described in section 170(b)(1)(A)(ii) or (iv) that are tax exempt under section 501(a) or whose income is excluded from taxation under section 115.

Form 1023-EZ Instructions

		Yes	No

15.	**Are you applying for exemption as a qualified charitable risk pool under section 501(n)?**
	
	A qualified charitable risk pool is treated as organized and operated exclusively for charitable purposes. Check the appropriate box to indicate whether you are a charitable risk pool. A qualified charitable risk pool is an organization that:
	
	1. Is organized and operated only to pool insurable risks of its members (not including risks related to medical malpractice) and to provide information to its members about loss control and risk management,
	
	2. Consists only of members that are section 501(c)(3) organizations exempt from tax under section 501(a),
	
	3. Is organized under state law authorizing this type of risk pooling,
	
	4. Is exempt from state income tax (or will be after qualifying as a section 501(c)(3) organization),
	
	5. Has obtained at least $1,000,000 in startup capital from nonmember charitable organizations,
	
	6. Is controlled by a board of directors elected by its members, and
	
	7. Is organized under documents requiring that:
	
	  a. Each member be a section 501(c)(3) organization exempt from tax under section 501(a),
	
	  b. Each member that receives a final determination that it no longer qualifies under section 501(c)(3) notify the pool immediately, and
	
	  c. Each insurance policy issued by the pool provide that it will not cover events occurring after a final determination described in (b).
		☐ Yes	☒ No

Form 1023-EZ Instructions   -15-

16.	Are you requesting classification as a supporting organization under section 509(a)(3)?	☐ Yes	☒ No
	A supporting organization (as defined in section 509(a)(3)) differs from the other types of public charities described in section 509. Instead of describing an organization that conducts a particular kind of activity or that receives financial support from the general public, section 509(a)(3) describes organizations that have established certain relationships in support of public charities described in section 509(a)(1) or 509(a)(2). Thus, an organization can qualify as a supporting organization (and not be classified as a private foundation) even though it may be funded by a single donor, family, or corporation. This kind of funding ordinarily would indicate private foundation status, but a section 509(a)(3) organization has limited purposes and activities, and gives up a significant degree of independence. A supporting organization is an organization that:		
	1. Is organized and operated exclusively for the benefit of, to perform the functions of, or to carry out the purposes of one or more specified organizations as described in section 509(a)(1) or 509(a)(2). These section 509(a)(1) and 509(a)(2) organizations are commonly called publicly supported organizations.		
	2. Has one of three types of relationships with one or more organizations described in section 509(a)(1) or 509(a)(2). It must be:		
	a. Operated, supervised, or controlled by one or more section 509(a)(1) or 509(a)(2) organizations (Type I supporting organization);		
	b. Supervised or controlled in connection with one or more section 509(a)(1) or 509(a)(2) organizations (Type II supporting organization); or		
	c. Operated in connection with one or more section 509(a)(1) or 509(a)(2) organizations (Type III supporting organization).		
	3. Is not controlled directly or indirectly by disqualified persons (as defined in section 4946) other than foundation managers and other than one or more organizations described in section 509(a)(1) or 509(a)(2).		
	See Publication 557 for more information.		
17.	Is a substantial purpose of your activities to provide assistance to individuals through credit counseling activities such as budgeting, personal finance, financial literacy, mortgage foreclosure assistance, or other consumer credit areas?	☐ Yes	☒ No
	These activities involve the education of the consumer on budgeting, personal finance, financial literacy, mortgage foreclosure assistance, or other consumer credit areas. It may also involve assisting the consumer in consolidating debt and negotiating between debtors and creditors to lower interest rates and waive late and over-limit fees.		
18.	Do you or will you invest 5% or more of your total assets in securities or funds that are not publicly traded?	☐ Yes	☒ No
19.	Do you participate, or intend to participate, in partnerships (including entities treated as partnerships for federal tax purposes) in which you share profits and losses with partners other than section 501(c)(3) organizations?	☐ Yes	☒ No
20.	Do you sell, or intend to sell carbon credits or carbon offsets?	☐ Yes	☒ No
21.	Are you a Health Maintenance Organization (HMO)?	☐ Yes	☒ No

22.	**Are you an Accountable Care Organization (ACO), or do you engage in or intend to engage in ACO activities?** ACOs are entities formed by groups of physicians, hospitals, and other health care service providers and suppliers to manage and coordinate the care provided to patients. For a discussion of tax law issues relating to ACOs, see Notice 2011-20 and FS-2011-11, available at *www.irs.gov/uac/Tax-Exempt-Organizations-Participating-in-the-Medicare-Shared-Savings-Program-through-Accountable-Care-Organizations*.	☐ Yes	☒ No
23.	**Do you maintain or intend to maintain one or more donor advised funds?** In general, a donor advised fund is a fund or account that is owned and controlled by the organization but that is separately identified by reference to contributions of a donor or donors and with respect to which a donor (or any person appointed or designated by the donor) has or expects to have advisory privileges concerning the distribution or investment of amounts held in the fund or account by reason of the donor's status as a donor. For additional information, see Publication 557. Check "No" if you are a governmental unit referred to in section 170(c)(1) or a private foundation referred to in section 509(a).	☐ Yes	☒ No
24.	**Are you organized and operated exclusively for testing for public safety and requesting a foundation classification under section 509(a)(4)?** Generally, these organizations test consumer products to determine their acceptability for use by the general public.	☐ Yes	☒ No
25.	**Are you requesting classification as a private operating foundation?** Private foundations lack general public support. What distinguishes a private operating foundation from other private foundations is that it engages directly in the active conduct of charitable, religious, educational, and similar activities (as opposed to indirectly carrying out these activities by providing grants to individuals or other organizations). Private operating foundations are subject to more favorable rules than other private foundations in terms of charitable contribution deductions and attracting grants from private foundations. However, to be classified as a private operating foundation, an organization must meet certain tests. Additional information about private operating foundations is available at *www.irs.gov/Charities-&-Non-Profits/Private-Foundations/Private-Operating-Foundations*.	☐ Yes	☒ No
26.	**Are you applying for retroactive reinstatement of exemption under section 5 or 6 of Rev. Proc. 2014-11, after being automatically revoked?** Only organizations applying for reinstatement under section 4 or 7 of Rev. Proc. 2014-11 may use Form 1023-EZ. If you are applying for retroactive reinstatement under section 5 or 6 of Rev. Proc. 2014-11, you must submit the full Form 1023 along with the appropriate reasonable cause statement and a statement confirming you have filed the required annual returns as described in the revenue procedure.	☐ Yes	☒ No

Form 1023-EZ Instructions   -17-

National Taxonomy of Exempt Entities (NTEE) Codes.

Arts, Culture, and Humanities

A01	Alliance/Advocacy Organizations
A02	Management & Technical Assistance
A03	Professional Societies, Associations
A05	Research Institutes and/or Public Policy Analysis
A11	Single Organization Support
A12	Fund Raising and/or Fund Distribution
A19	Nonmonetary Support N.E.C.*
A20	Arts, Cultural Organizations - Multipurpose
A23	Cultural, Ethnic Awareness
A25	Arts Education
A26	Arts Council/Agency
A30	Media, Communications Organizations
A31	Film, Video
A32	Television
A33	Printing, Publishing
A34	Radio
A40	Visual Arts Organizations
A50	Museum, Museum Activities
A51	Art Museums
A52	Children's Museums
A54	History Museums
A56	Natural History, Natural Science Museums
A57	Science and Technology Museums
A60	Performing Arts Organizations
A61	Performing Arts Centers
A62	Dance
A63	Ballet
A65	Theater
A68	Music
A69	Symphony Orchestras
A6A	Opera
A6B	Singing, Choral
A6C	Music Groups, Bands, Ensembles
A6E	Performing Arts Schools
A70	Humanities Organizations
A80	Historical Societies, Related Historical Activities
A84	Commemorative Events
A90	Arts Service Organizations and Activities
A99	Arts, Culture, and Humanities N.E.C.

Education

B01	Alliance/Advocacy Organizations
B02	Management & Technical Assistance
B03	Professional Societies, Associations
B05	Research Institutes and/or Public Policy Analysis
B11	Single Organization Support
B12	Fund Raising and/or Fund Distribution
B19	Nonmonetary Support N.E.C.
B20	Elementary, Secondary Education, K - 12
B21	Kindergarten, Preschool, Nursery School, Early Admissions
B24	Primary, Elementary Schools
B25	Secondary, High School
B28	Specialized Education Institutions
B30	Vocational, Technical Schools
B40	Higher Education Institutions
B41	Community or Junior Colleges
B42	Undergraduate College (4-year)
B43	University or Technological Institute
B50	Graduate, Professional Schools (Separate Entities)
B60	Adult, Continuing Education
B70	Libraries
B80	Student Services, Organizations of Students
B82	Scholarships, Student Financial Aid Services, Awards
B83	Student Sororities, Fraternities
B84	Alumni Associations
B90	Educational Services and Schools - Other
B92	Remedial Reading, Reading Encouragement
B94	Parent/Teacher Group
B99	Education N.E.C.

Environmental Quality, Protection, and Beautification

C01	Alliance/Advocacy Organizations
C02	Management & Technical Assistance
C03	Professional Societies, Associations
C05	Research Institutes and/or Public Policy Analysis
C11	Single Organization Support
C12	Fund Raising and/or Fund Distribution
C19	Nonmonetary Support N.E.C.
C20	Pollution Abatement and Control Services
C27	Recycling Programs
C30	Natural Resources Conservation and Protection
C32	Water Resource, Wetlands Conservation and Management
C34	Land Resources Conservation
C35	Energy Resources Conservation and Development
C36	Forest Conservation
C40	Botanical, Horticultural, and Landscape Services
C41	Botanical Gardens, Arboreta and Botanical Organizations
C42	Garden Club, Horticultural Program
C50	Environmental Beautification and Aesthetics
C60	Environmental Education and Outdoor Survival Programs
C99	Environmental Quality, Protection, and Beautification N.E.C.

Animal-Related

D01	Alliance/Advocacy Organizations
D02	Management & Technical Assistance
D03	Professional Societies, Associations
D05	Research Institutes and/or Public Policy Analysis
D11	Single Organization Support
D12	Fund Raising and/or Fund Distribution
D19	Nonmonetary Support N.E.C.
D20	Animal Protection and Welfare
D30	Wildlife Preservation, Protection
D31	Protection of Endangered Species
D32	Bird Sanctuary, Preserve
D33	Fisheries Resources
D34	Wildlife Sanctuary, Refuge
D40	Veterinary Services
D50	Zoo, Zoological Society
D60	Other Services - Specialty Animals
D61	Animal Training, Behavior
D99	Animal-Related N.E.C.

Health - General and Rehabilitative

E01	Alliance/Advocacy Organizations
E02	Management & Technical Assistance
E03	Professional Societies, Associations
E05	Research Institutes and/or Public Policy Analysis
E11	Single Organization Support
E12	Fund Raising and/or Fund Distribution
E19	Nonmonetary Support N.E.C.
E20	Hospitals and Related Primary Medical Care Facilities
E21	Community Health Systems
E22	Hospital, General
E24	Hospital, Specialty
E30	Health Treatment Facilities, Primarily Outpatient
E31	Group Health Practice (Health Maintenance Organizations)
E32	Ambulatory Health Center, Community Clinic
E40	Reproductive Health Care Facilities and Allied Services
E42	Family Planning Centers
E50	Rehabilitative Medical Services
E60	Health Support Services
E61	Blood Supply Related
E62	Ambulance, Emergency Medical Transport Services
E65	Organ and Tissue Banks
E70	Public Health Program (Includes General Health and Wellness Promotion Services)
E80	Health, General and Financing
E86	Patient Services - Entertainment, Recreation
E90	Nursing Services (General)
E91	Nursing, Convalescent Facilities
E92	Home Health Care
E99	Health - General and Rehabilitative N.E.C.

Mental Health, Crisis Intervention

F01	Alliance/Advocacy Organizations
F02	Management & Technical Assistance
F03	Professional Societies, Associations
F05	Research Institutes and/or Public Policy Analysis
F11	Single Organization Support
F12	Fund Raising and/or Fund Distribution
F19	Nonmonetary Support N.E.C.
F20	Alcohol, Drug and Substance Abuse, Dependency Prevention and Treatment
F21	Alcohol, Drug Abuse, Prevention Only
F22	Alcohol, Drug Abuse, Treatment Only
F30	Mental Health Treatment - Multipurpose and N.E.C.
F31	Psychiatric, Mental Health Hospital
F32	Community Mental Health Center
F33	Group Home, Residential Treatment Facility - Mental Health Related
F40	Hot Line, Crisis Intervention Services
F42	Rape Victim Services
F50	Addictive Disorders N.E.C.
F52	Smoking Addiction
F53	Eating Disorder, Addiction
F54	Gambling Addiction
F60	Counseling, Support Groups
F70	Mental Health Disorders
F80	Mental Health Association, Multipurpose
F99	Mental Health, Crisis Intervention N.E.C.

Diseases, Disorders, Medical Disciplines

G01	Alliance/Advocacy Organizations
G02	Management & Technical Assistance
G03	Professional Societies, Associations
G05	Research Institutes and/or Public Policy Analysis
G11	Single Organization Support
G12	Fund Raising and/or Fund Distribution
G19	Nonmonetary Support N.E.C.
G20	Birth Defects and Genetic Diseases
G25	Down Syndrome
G30	Cancer
G40	Diseases of Specific Organs
G41	Eye Diseases, Blindness and Vision Impairments
G42	Ear and Throat Diseases
G43	Heart and Circulatory System Diseases, Disorders
G44	Kidney Disease
G45	Lung Disease
G48	Brain Disorders
G50	Nerve, Muscle and Bone Diseases
G51	Arthritis
G54	Epilepsy
G60	Allergy Related Diseases G61 Asthma
G70	Digestive Diseases, Disorders
G80	Specifically Named Diseases
G81	AIDS
G83	Alzheimer's Disease
G84	Autism
G90	Medical Disciplines
G92	Biomedicine, Bioengineering
G94	Geriatrics
G96	Neurology, Neuroscience
G98	Pediatrics
G9B	Surgery
G99	Diseases, Disorders, Medical Disciplines N.E.C.

Medical Research

H01	Alliance/Advocacy Organizations
H02	Management & Technical Assistance
H03	Professional Societies, Associations
H05	Research Institutes and/or Public Policy Analysis
H11	Single Organization Support
H12	Fund Raising and/or Fund Distribution
H19	Nonmonetary Support N.E.C.
H20	Birth Defects, Genetic Diseases Research
H25	Down Syndrome Research
H30	Cancer Research
H40	Specific Organ Research
H41	Eye Research
H42	Ear and Throat Research
H43	Heart, Circulatory Research
H44	Kidney Research
H45	Lung Research
H48	Brain Disorders Research
H50	Nerve, Muscle, Bone Research
H51	Arthritis Research
H54	Epilepsy Research
H60	Allergy Related Disease Research
H61	Asthma Research
H70	Digestive Disease, Disorder Research
H80	Specifically Named Diseases Research
H81	AIDS Research
H83	Alzheimer's Disease Research
H84	Autism Research
H90	Medical Specialty Research
H92	Biomedicine, Bioengineering Research
H94	Geriatrics Research
H96	Neurology, Neuroscience Research
H98	Pediatrics Research
H9B	Surgery Research
H99	Medical Research N.E.C.

Crime, Legal Related

I01	Alliance/Advocacy Organizations
I02	Management & Technical Assistance
I03	Professional Societies, Associations
I05	Research Institutes and/or Public Policy Analysis
I11	Single Organization Support
I12	Fund Raising and/or Fund Distribution
I19	Nonmonetary Support N.E.C.
I20	Crime Prevention N.E.C.
I21	Delinquency Prevention
I23	Drunk Driving Related
I30	Correctional Facilities N.E.C.
I31	Transitional Care, Half-Way House for Offenders, Ex-Offenders
I40	Rehabilitation Services for Offenders
I43	Services to Prisoners and Families - Multipurpose
I44	Prison Alternatives
I50	Administration of Justice, Courts
I51	Dispute Resolution, Mediation Services
I60	Law Enforcement Agencies (Police Departments)
I70	Protection Against, Prevention of Neglect, Abuse, Exploitation
I71	Spouse Abuse, Prevention of
I72	Child Abuse, Prevention of
I73	Sexual Abuse, Prevention of
I80	Legal Services
I83	Public Interest Law, Litigation
I99	Crime, Legal Related N.E.C.

Employment, Job Related

J01	Alliance/Advocacy Organizations
J02	Management & Technical Assistance
J03	Professional Societies, Associations
J05	Research Institutes and/or Public Policy Analysis
J11	Single Organization Support
J12	Fund Raising and/or Fund Distribution
J19	Nonmonetary Support N.E.C.
J20	Employment Procurement Assistance, Job Training
J21	Vocational Counseling, Guidance and Testing
J22	Vocational Training
J30	Vocational Rehabilitation
J32	Goodwill Industries
J33	Sheltered Remunerative Employment, Work Activity Center N.E.C.
J40	Labor Unions, Organizations
J99	Employment, Job Related N.E.C.

Food, Agriculture, and Nutrition

K01	Alliance/Advocacy Organizations
K02	Management & Technical Assistance
K03	Professional Societies, Associations
K05	Research Institutes and/or Public Policy Analysis
K11	Single Organization Support
K12	Fund Raising and/or Fund Distribution
K19	Nonmonetary Support N.E.C.
K20	Agricultural Programs
K25	Farmland Preservation
K26	Livestock Breeding, Development, Management
K28	Farm Bureau, Grange
K30	Food Service, Free Food Distribution Programs
K31	Food Banks, Food Pantries
K34	Congregate Meals
K35	Eatery, Agency, Organization Sponsored
K36	Meals on Wheels
K40	Nutrition Programs
K50	Home Economics
K99	Food, Agriculture, and Nutrition N.E.C.

Housing, Shelter

L01	Alliance/Advocacy Organizations
L02	Management & Technical Assistance
L03	Professional Societies, Associations
L05	Research Institutes and/or Public Policy Analysis
L11	Single Organization Support
L12	Fund Raising and/or Fund Distribution
L19	Nonmonetary Support N.E.C.
L20	Housing Development, Construction, Management
L21	Public Housing Facilities
L22	Senior Citizens' Housing/ Retirement Communities
L25	Housing Rehabilitation
L30	Housing Search Assistance
L40	Low-Cost Temporary Housing
L41	Homeless, Temporary Shelter For
L50	Housing Owners, Renters Organizations
L80	Housing Support Services -- Other
L81	Home Improvement and Repairs
L82	Housing Expense Reduction Support
L99	Housing, Shelter N.E.C.

Public Safety, Disaster Preparedness, and Relief

M01	Alliance/Advocacy Organizations
M02	Management & Technical Assistance
M03	Professional Societies, Associations
M05	Research Institutes and/or Public Policy Analysis
M11	Single Organization Support
M12	Fund Raising and/or Fund Distribution
M19	Nonmonetary Support N.E.C.
M20	Disaster Preparedness and Relief Services
M23	Search and Rescue Squads, Services
M24	Fire Prevention, Protection, Control
M40	Safety Education
M41	First Aid Training, Services
M42	Automotive Safety
M99	Public Safety, Disaster Preparedness, and Relief N.E.C.

Recreation, Sports, Leisure, Athletics

N01	Alliance/Advocacy Organizations
N02	Management & Technical Assistance
N03	Professional Societies, Associations
N05	Research Institutes and/or Public Policy Analysis
N11	Single Organization Support
N12	Fund Raising and/or Fund Distribution
N19	Nonmonetary Support N.E.C.
N20	Recreational and Sporting Camps
N30	Physical Fitness and Community Recreational Facilities
N31	Community Recreational Centers
N32	Parks and Playgrounds
N40	Sports Training Facilities, Agencies
N50	Recreational, Pleasure, or Social Club
N52	Fairs, County and Other
N60	Amateur Sports Clubs, Leagues, N.E.C.
N61	Fishing, Hunting Clubs
N62	Basketball
N63	Baseball, Softball
N64	Soccer Clubs, Leagues
N65	Football Clubs, Leagues
N66	Tennis, Racquet Sports Clubs, Leagues
N67	Swimming, Water Recreation
N68	Winter Sports (Snow and Ice)
N69	Equestrian, Riding
N6A	Golf
N70	Amateur Sports Competitions
N71	Olympics Committees and Related International Competitions
N72	Special Olympics
N80	Professional Athletic Leagues
N99	Recreation, Sports, Leisure, Athletics N.E.C.

Youth Development

O01	Alliance/Advocacy Organizations
O02	Management & Technical Assistance
O03	Professional Societies, Associations
O05	Research Institutes and/or Public Policy Analysis
O11	Single Organization Support
O12	Fund Raising and/or Fund Distribution
O19	Nonmonetary Support N.E.C.
O20	Youth Centers, Clubs, Multipurpose
O21	Boys Clubs
O22	Girls Clubs O23 Boys and Girls Clubs (Combined)
O30	Adult, Child Matching Programs
O31	Big Brothers, Big Sisters
O40	Scouting Organizations
O41	Boy Scouts of America
O42	Girl Scouts of the U.S.A.
O43	Camp Fire
O50	Youth Development Programs, Other
O51	Youth Community Service Clubs
O52	Youth Development - Agricultural
O53	Youth Development - Business
O54	Youth Development - Citizenship Programs
O55	Youth Development - Religious Leadership
O99	Youth Development N.E.C.

Human Services - Multipurpose and Other

P01	Alliance/Advocacy Organizations
P02	Management & Technical Assistance
P03	Professional Societies, Associations
P05	Research Institutes and/or Public Policy Analysis
P11	Single Organization Support
P12	Fund Raising and/or Fund Distribution
P19	Nonmonetary Support N.E.C.
P20	Human Service Organizations - Multipurpose
P21	American Red Cross
P22	Urban League
P24	Salvation Army
P26	Volunteers of America
P27	Young Men's or Women's Associations (YMCA, YWCA, YWHA, YMHA)
P28	Neighborhood Centers, Settlement Houses
P29	Thrift Shops
P30	Children's, Youth Services
P31	Adoption
P32	Foster Care
P33	Child Day Care
P40	Family Services
P42	Single Parent Agencies, Services
P43	Family Violence Shelters, Services
P44	Homemaker, Home Health Aide
P45	Family Services, Adolescent Parents
P46	Family Counseling
P50	Personal Social Services
P51	Financial Counseling, Money Management
P52	Transportation, Free or Subsidized
P58	Gift Distribution
P60	Emergency Assistance (Food, Clothing, Cash)
P61	Travelers' Aid
P62	Victims' Services
P70	Residential, Custodial Care
P72	Half-Way House (Short-Term Residential Care)
P73	Group Home (Long Term)
P74	Hospice
P75	Senior Continuing Care Communities
P80	Services to Promote the Independence of Specific Populations
P81	Senior Centers, Services
P82	Developmentally Disabled Centers, Services
P84	Ethnic, Immigrant Centers, Services
P85	Homeless Persons Centers, Services
P86	Blind/Visually Impaired Centers, Services
P87	Deaf/Hearing Impaired Centers, Services
P99	Human Services - Multipurpose and Other N.E.C.

International, Foreign Affairs, and National Security

Q01	Alliance/Advocacy Organizations
Q02	Management & Technical Assistance
Q03	Professional Societies, Associations
Q05	Research Institutes and/or Public Policy Analysis
Q11	Single Organization Support
Q12	Fund Raising and/or Fund Distribution
Q19	Nonmonetary Support N.E.C.
Q20	Promotion of International Understanding
Q21	International Cultural Exchange
Q22	International Student Exchange and Aid
Q23	International Exchanges, N.E.C.
Q30	International Development, Relief Services
Q31	International Agricultural Development
Q32	International Economic Development
Q33	International Relief
Q40	International Peace and Security
Q41	Arms Control, Peace Organizations
Q42	United Nations Association
Q43	National Security, Domestic
Q70	International Human Rights
Q71	International Migration, Refugee Issues
Q99	International, Foreign Affairs, and National Security N.E.C.

Civil Rights, Social Action, Advocacy

R01	Alliance/Advocacy Organizations
R02	Management & Technical Assistance
R03	Professional Societies, Associations
R05	Research Institutes and/or Public Policy Analysis
R11	Single Organization Support
R12	Fund Raising and/or Fund Distribution
R19	Nonmonetary Support N.E.C.
R20	Civil Rights, Advocacy for Specific Groups
R22	Minority Rights
R23	Disabled Persons' Rights
R24	Women's Rights
R25	Seniors' Rights
R26	Lesbian, Gay Rights
R30	Intergroup, Race Relations
R40	Voter Education, Registration
R60	Civil Liberties Advocacy
R61	Reproductive Rights
R62	Right to Life
R63	Censorship, Freedom of Speech and Press Issues
R67	Right to Die, Euthanasia Issues
R99	Civil Rights, Social Action, Advocacy N.E.C.

Community Improvement, Capacity Building

S01	Alliance/Advocacy Organizations
S02	Management & Technical Assistance
S03	Professional Societies, Associations
S05	Research Institutes and/or Public Policy Analysis
S11	Single Organization Support
S12	Fund Raising and/or Fund Distribution
S19	Nonmonetary Support N.E.C.
S20	Community, Neighborhood Development, Improvement (General)
S21	Community Coalitions
S22	Neighborhood, Block Associations
S30	Economic Development
S31	Urban, Community Economic Development
S32	Rural Development
S40	Business and Industry
S41	Promotion of Business
S43	Management Services for Small Business, Entrepreneurs
S46	Boards of Trade
S47	Real Estate Organizations
S50	Nonprofit Management
S80	Community Service Clubs
S81	Women's Service Clubs
S82	Men's Service Clubs
S99	Community Improvement, Capacity Building N.E.C.

Philanthropy, Voluntarism, and Grantmaking Foundations

T01	Alliance/Advocacy Organizations
T02	Management & Technical Assistance
T03	Professional Societies, Associations
T05	Research Institutes and/or Public Policy Analysis
T11	Single Organization Support
T12	Fund Raising and/or Fund Distribution
T19	Nonmonetary Support N.E.C.
T20	Private Grantmaking Foundations
T21	Corporate Foundations
T22	Private Independent Foundations
T23	Private Operating Foundations
T30	Public Foundations
T31	Community Foundations
T40	Voluntarism Promotion
T50	Philanthropy, Charity, Voluntarism Promotion, General
T70	Fund Raising Organizations That Cross Categories
T90	Named Trusts/Foundations N.E.C.
T99	Philanthropy, Voluntarism, and Grantmaking Foundations N.E.C.

Science and Technology Research Institutes, Services

U01	Alliance/Advocacy Organizations
U02	Management & Technical Assistance
U03	Professional Societies, Associations
U05	Research Institutes and/or Public Policy Analysis
U11	Single Organization Support
U12	Fund Raising and/or Fund Distribution
U19	Nonmonetary Support N.E.C.
U20	Science, General
U21	Marine Science and Oceanography
U30	Physical Sciences, Earth Sciences Research and Promotion
U31	Astronomy
U33	Chemistry, Chemical Engineering
U34	Mathematics
U36	Geology
U40	Engineering and Technology Research, Services
U41	Computer Science
U42	Engineering
U50	Biological, Life Science Research
U99	Science and Technology Research Institutes, Services N.E.C.

Social Science Research Institutes, Services

V01	Alliance/Advocacy Organizations
V02	Management & Technical Assistance
V03	Professional Societies, Associations
V05	Research Institutes and/or Public Policy Analysis
V11	Single Organization Support
V12	Fund Raising and/or Fund Distribution
V19	Nonmonetary Support N.E.C.
V20	Social Science Institutes, Services
V21	Anthropology, Sociology
V22	Economics (as a social science)
V23	Behavioral Science
V24	Political Science
V25	Population Studies
V26	Law, International Law, Jurisprudence
V30	Interdisciplinary Research
V31	Black Studies
V32	Women's Studies
V33	Ethnic Studies
V34	Urban Studies
V35	International Studies
V36	Gerontology (as a social science)
V37	Labor Studies V99 Social Science Research Institutes, Services N.E.C.

Public, Society Benefit - Multipurpose and Other

W01	Alliance/Advocacy Organizations
W02	Management & Technical Assistance
W03	Professional Societies, Associations
W05	Research Institutes and/or Public Policy Analysis
W11	Single Organization Support
W12	Fund Raising and/or Fund Distribution
W19	Nonmonetary Support N.E.C.
W20	Government and Public Administration
W22	Public Finance, Taxation, Monetary Policy
W24	Citizen Participation
W30	Military, Veterans' Organizations
W40	Public Transportation Systems, Services
W50	Telephone, Telegraph and Telecommunication Services
W60	Financial Institutions, Services (Non-Government Related)
W61	Credit Unions
W70	Leadership Development
W80	Public Utilities
W90	Consumer Protection, Safety
W99	Public, Society Benefit - Multipurpose and Other N.E.C.

Religion Related, Spiritual Development

X01	Alliance/Advocacy Organizations
X02	Management & Technical Assistance
X03	Professional Societies, Associations
X05	Research Institutes and/or Public Policy Analysis
X11	Single Organization Support
X12	Fund Raising and/or Fund Distribution
X19	Nonmonetary Support N.E.C.
X20	Christian
X21	Protestant
X22	Roman Catholic
X30	Jewish
X40	Islamic
X50	Buddhist
X70	Hindu
X80	Religious Media, Communications Organizations
X81	Religious Film, Video
X82	Religious Television
X83	Religious Printing, Publishing
X84	Religious Radio
X90	Interfaith Issues
X99	Religion Related, Spiritual Development N.E.C.

Mutual/Membership Benefit Organizations, Other

Y01	Alliance/Advocacy Organizations
Y02	Management & Technical Assistance
Y03	Professional Societies, Associations
Y05	Research Institutes and/or Public Policy Analysis
Y11	Single Organization Support
Y12	Fund Raising and/or Fund Distribution
Y19	Nonmonetary Support N.E.C.
Y20	Insurance Providers, Services
Y22	Local Benevolent Life Insurance Associations, Mutual Irrigation and Telephone Companies, and Like Organizations
Y23	Mutual Insurance Company or Association
Y24	Supplemental Unemployment Compensation
Y25	State-Sponsored Worker's Compensation Reinsurance Organizations
Y30	Pension and Retirement Funds
Y33	Teachers Retirement Fund Association
Y34	Employee Funded Pension Trust
Y35	Multi-Employer Pension Plans
Y40	Fraternal Beneficiary Societies
Y42	Domestic Fraternal Societies
Y43	Voluntary Employees Beneficiary Associations (Non-Government)
Y44	Voluntary Employees Beneficiary Associations (Government)
Y50	Cemeteries, Burial Services
Y99	Mutual/Membership Benefit Organizations, Other N.E.C.

Unknown

Z99	Unknown

You must complete the Form 1023-EZ Eligibility Worksheet in the Instructions for Form 1023-EZ to determine if you are eligible to file this form. Form 1023-EZ is filed electronically **only** on Pay.gov. Go to www.irs.gov/form1023ez for additional filing information.

| Form **1023-EZ**
(June 2014)

Department of the Treasury
Internal Revenue Service | **Streamlined Application for Recognition of Exemption Under Section 501(c)(3) of the Internal Revenue Code**

▶ Do not enter social security numbers on this form as it may be made public.
▶ Information about Form 1023-EZ and its separate instructions is at *www.irs.gov/form1023.* | OMB No. 1545-0056

Note: *If exempt status is approved, this application will be open for public inspection.* |

☐ Check this box to attest that you have completed the Form 1023-EZ Eligibility Worksheet in the current instructions, are eligible to apply for exemption using Form 1023-EZ, and have read and understand the requirements to be exempt under section 501(c)(3).

Part I Identification of Applicant

1a Full Name of Organization: My Nonprofit, Inc.

b Address (number, street, and room/suite). If a P.O. box, see instructions. 123 Need Street	**c** City Any Town	**d** State GA	**e** Zip Code + 4 12345

2 Employer Identification Number	**3** Month Tax Year Ends (MM) December	**4** Person to Contact if More Information is Needed Mr. & Mrs. Concerned

5 Contact Telephone Number 404-123-4567	**6** Fax Number (optional)	**7** User Fee Submitted

8 List the names, titles, and mailing addresses of your officers, directors, and/or trustees. (If you have more than five, see instructions.)

First Name: Ima	Last Name: Visionary	Title: President	
Street Address: 123 My Street	City: My City	State: GA	Zip Code + 4: 12345
First Name:	Last Name:	Title:	
Street Address:	City:	State:	Zip Code + 4:
First Name:	Last Name:	Title:	
Street Address:	City:	State:	Zip Code + 4:
First Name:	Last Name:	Title:	
Street Address:	City:	State:	Zip Code + 4:
First Name:	Last Name:	Title:	
Street Address:	City:	State:	Zip Code + 4:

9 a Organization's Website (if available): www.helpinghumanity.org

b Organization's Email (optional):

Part II Organizational Structure

1 To file this form, you must be a corporation, an unincorporated association, or a trust. **Check the box** for the type of organization.

☒ Corporation   ☐ Unincorporated association   ☐ Trust

2 ☐ **Check this box** to attest that you have the organizing document necessary for the organizational structure indicated above. (See the instructions for an explanation of **necessary organizing documents**.)   01/01/2016

3 Date incorporated if a corporation, or formed if other than a corporation (MMDDYYYY).

4 State of incorporation or other formation: Georgia

5 Section 501(c)(3) requires that your organizing document must limit your purposes to one or more exempt purposes within section 501(c)(3).

☒ **Check this box** to attest that your organizing document contains this limitation.

6 Section 501(c)(3) requires that your organizing document must not expressly empower you to engage, otherwise than as an insubstantial part of your activities, in activities that in themselves are not in furtherance of one or more exempt purposes.

☒ **Check this box** to attest that your organizing document does not expressly empower you to engage, otherwise than as an insubstantial part of your activities, in activities that in themselves are not in furtherance of one or more exempt purposes.

7 Section 501(c)(3) requires that your organizing document must provide that upon dissolution, your remaining assets be used exclusively for section 501(c)(3) exempt purposes. Depending on your entity type and the state in which you are formed, this requirement may be satisfied by operation of state law.

☒ **Check this box** to attest that your organizing document contains the dissolution provision required under section 501(c)(3) or that you do not need an express dissolution provision in your organizing document because you rely on the operation of state law in the state in which you are formed for your dissolution provision.

For Paperwork Reduction Act Notice, see the instructions.   Catalog No. 66267N   Form **1023-EZ** (6-2014)

You must complete the Form 1023-EZ Eligibility Worksheet in the Instructions for Form 1023-EZ to determine if you are eligible to file this form. Form 1023-EZ is filed electronically **only** on Pay.gov. Go to www.irs.gov/form1023ez for additional filing information.

Form 1023-EZ (6-2014)   Page **2**

Part III   Your Specific Activities

1 Enter the appropriate 3-character NTEE Code that best describes your activities (See the instructions): _____

2 To qualify for exemption as a section 501(c)(3) organization, you must be organized and operated exclusively to further one or more of the following purposes. By checking the box or boxes below, you attest that you are organized and operated exclusively to further the purposes indicated. **Check all that apply.**

- [X] Charitable
- [ ] Religious
- [ ] Educational
- [ ] Scientific
- [ ] Literary
- [ ] Testing for public safety
- [ ] To foster national or international amateur sports competition
- [ ] Prevention of cruelty to children or animals

3 To qualify for exemption as a section 501(c)(3) organization, you must:

- Refrain from supporting or opposing candidates in political campaigns in any way.
- Ensure that your net earnings do not inure in whole or in part to the benefit of private shareholders or individuals (that is, board members, officers, key management employees, or other insiders).
- Not further non-exempt purposes (such as purposes that benefit private interests) more than insubstantially.
- Not be organized or operated for the primary purpose of conducting a trade or business that is not related to your exempt purpose(s).
- Not devote more than an insubstantial part of your activities attempting to influence legislation or, if you made a section 501(h) election, not normally make expenditures in excess of expenditure limitations outlined in section 501(h).
- Not provide commercial-type insurance as a substantial part of your activities.

- [ ] **Check this box** to attest that you have not conducted and will not conduct activities that violate these prohibitions and restrictions.

4 Do you or will you attempt to influence legislation? . . . . [ ] Yes [X] No
   (If yes, consider filing Form 5768. See the instructions for more details.)

5 Do you or will you pay compensation to any of your officers, directors, or trustees? . . . . [ ] Yes [X] No
   (Refer to the instructions for a definition of **compensation**.)

6 Do you or will you donate funds to or pay expenses for individual(s)? . . . . [ ] Yes [x] No

7 Do you or will you conduct activities or provide grants or other assistance to individual(s) or organization(s) outside the United States? . . . . [ ] Yes [X] No

8 Do you or will you engage in financial transactions (for example, loans, payments, rents, etc.) with any of your officers, directors, or trustees, or any entities they own or control? . . . . [ ] Yes [X] No

9 Do you or will you have unrelated business gross income of $1,000 or more during a tax year? . . . . [ ] Yes [X] No

10 Do you or will you operate bingo or other gaming activities? . . . . [ ] Yes [X] No

11 Do you or will you provide disaster relief? . . . . [ ] Yes [x] No

Part IV   Foundation Classification

Part IV is designed to classify you as an organization that is either a private foundation or a public charity. Public charity status is a more favorable tax status than private foundation status.

1 If you qualify for public charity status, check the appropriate box (1a – 1c below) and skip to **Part V** below.

a [X] **Check this box** to attest that you normally receive at least one-third of your support from public sources or you normally receive at least 10 percent of your support from public sources and you have other characteristics of a publicly supported organization. **Sections 509(a)(1) and 170(b)(1)(A)(vi)**.

b [ ] **Check this box** to attest that you normally receive more than one-third of your support from a combination of gifts, grants, contributions, membership fees, and gross receipts (from permitted sources) from activities related to your exempt functions and normally receive not more than one-third of your support from investment income and unrelated business taxable income. **Section 509(a)(2)**.

c [ ] **Check this box** to attest that you are operated for the benefit of a college or university that is owned or operated by a governmental unit. **Sections 509(a)(1) and 170(b)(1)(A)(iv)**.

2 If you are not described in items **1a – 1c** above, you are a private foundation. As a private foundation, you are required by section 508(e) to have specific provisions in your organizing document, unless you rely on the operation of state law in the state in which you were formed to meet these requirements. These specific provisions require that you operate to avoid liability for private foundation excise taxes under sections 4941-4945.

- [ ] **Check this box** to attest that your organizing document contains the provisions required by section 508(e) or that your organizing document does not need to include the provisions required by section 508(e) because you rely on the operation of state law in your particular state to meet the requirements of section 508(e). (See the instructions for explanation of the section 508(e) requirements.)

Form **1023-EZ** (6-2014)

Form 1023-EZ (6-2014)

You must complete the Form 1023-EZ Eligibility Worksheet in the Instructions for Form 1023-EZ to determine if you are eligible to file this form. Form 1023-EZ is filed electronically **only** on Pay.gov. Go to www.irs.gov/form1023ez for additional filing information.

Page **3**

Part V   Reinstatement After Automatic Revocation

Complete this section only if you are applying for reinstatement of exemption after being automatically revoked for failure to file required annual returns or notices for three consecutive years, and you are applying for reinstatement under section 4 or 7 of Revenue Procedure 2014-11. (Check only one box.)

1   ☐ Check this box if you are seeking retroactive reinstatement under section 4 of Revenue Procedure 2014-11. By checking this box, you attest that you meet the specified requirements of section 4, that your failure to file was not intentional, and that you have put in place procedures to file required returns or notices in the future. (See the instructions for requirements.)

2   ☐ Check this box if you are seeking reinstatement under section 7 of Revenue Procedure 2014-11, effective the date you are filling this application.

Part VI   Signature   YOUR SIGNATURE

☒ I declare under the penalties of perjury that I am authorized to sign this application on behalf of the above organization and that I have examined this application, and to the best of my knowledge it is true, correct, and complete.

Your name	President
(Type name of signer)	(Type title or authority of signer)

PLEASE SIGN HERE ▶

Your signature	
(Signature of Officer, Director, Trustee, or other authorized official)	(Date)

Form **1023-EZ** (6-2014)

NOTE: Please keep in mind that this is a sample that will possibly apply to most start-up organizations.
If you have any questions, consult with qualified sources before filing.

Printed on recycled paper

25

Form **1023**
(Rev. June 2006)
Department of the Treasury
Internal Revenue Service

Application for Recognition of Exemption
Under Section 501(c)(3) of the Internal Revenue Code

OMB No. 1545-0056

Note: *If exempt status is approved, this application will be open for public inspection.*

Use the instructions to complete this application and for a definition of all **bold** items. For additional help, call IRS Exempt Organizations Customer Account Services toll-free at 1-877-829-5500. Visit our website at **www.irs.gov** for forms and publications. If the required information and documents are not submitted with payment of the appropriate user fee, the application may be returned to you.

Attach additional sheets to this application if you need more space to answer fully. Put your name and EIN on each sheet and identify each answer by Part and line number. Complete Parts I - XI of Form 1023 and submit only those Schedules (A through H) that apply to you.

Part I   Identification of Applicant

1 Full name of organization (exactly as it appears in your **organizing document**) Marrow For Life, Inc.	2 c/o Name (if applicable) Dan Moore
3 **Mailing address** (Number and street) (see instructions) Room/Suite 135 Auburn Ave.	4 Employer Identification Number (EIN) 20-4705699
City or town, state or country, and ZIP + 4 Atlanta, GA 30303	5 Month the annual accounting period ends (01 – 12) 12
6 Primary contact (officer, director, trustee, or **authorized representative**) a Name: **Dan Moore, Sr.**	b Phone: 404-523-2739
	c Fax: (optional) 404-523-3248

7 Are you represented by an authorized representative, such as an attorney or accountant? If "Yes," provide the authorized representative's name, and the name and address of the authorized representative's firm. Include a completed Form 2848, *Power of Attorney and Declaration of Representative*, with your application if you would like us to communicate with your representative.   ☐ Yes ☑ No

8 Was a person who is not one of your officers, directors, trustees, employees, or an authorized representative listed in line 7, paid, or promised payment, to help plan, manage, or advise you about the structure or activities of your organization, or about your financial or tax matters? If "Yes," provide the person's name, the name and address of the person's firm, the amounts paid or promised to be paid, and describe that person's role.   ☐ Yes ☑ No

9a Organization's website:

b Organization's email: (optional)

10 Certain organizations are not required to file an information return (Form 990 or Form 990-EZ). If you are granted tax-exemption, are you claiming to be excused from filing Form 990 or Form 990-EZ? If "Yes," explain. See the instructions for a description of organizations not required to file Form 990 or Form 990-EZ.   ☐ Yes ☑ No

11 Date incorporated if a corporation, or formed, if other than a corporation.   (MM/DD/YYYY)   **04** / **17** / **2006**

12 Were you formed under the laws of a **foreign country**? If "Yes," state the country.   ☐ Yes ☑ No

For Paperwork Reduction Act Notice, see page 24 of the instructions.   Cat. No. 17133K   Form **1023** (Rev. 6-2006)

Part II Organizational Structure

You must be a corporation (including a limited liability company), an unincorporated association, or a trust to be tax exempt. (See instructions.) DO NOT file this form unless you can check "Yes" on lines 1, 2, 3, or 4.

1 Are you a **corporation**? If "Yes," attach a copy of your articles of incorporation showing **certification of filing** with the appropriate state agency. Include copies of any amendments to your articles and be sure they also show state filing certification. ☑ Yes ☐ No

2 Are you a **limited liability company (LLC)**? If "Yes," attach a copy of your articles of organization showing certification of filing with the appropriate state agency. Also, if you adopted an operating agreement, attach a copy. Include copies of any amendments to your articles and be sure they show state filing certification. Refer to the instructions for circumstances when an LLC should not file its own exemption application. ☐ Yes ☑ No

3 Are you an **unincorporated association**? If "Yes," attach a copy of your articles of association, constitution, or other similar organizing document that is dated and includes at least two signatures. Include signed and dated copies of any amendments. ☐ Yes ☑ No

4a Are you a **trust**? If "Yes," attach a signed and dated copy of your trust agreement. Include signed and dated copies of any amendments. ☐ Yes ☑ No

b Have you been funded? If "No," explain how you are formed without anything of value placed in trust. ☐ Yes ☐ No

5 Have you adopted **bylaws**? If "Yes," attach a current copy showing date of adoption. If "No," explain how your officers, directors, or trustees are selected. ☑ Yes ☐ No

Part III Required Provisions in Your Organizing Document

The following questions are designed to ensure that when you file this application, your organizing document contains the required provisions to meet the organizational test under section 501(c)(3). Unless you can check the boxes in both lines 1 and 2, your organizing document does not meet the organizational test. **DO NOT file this application until you have amended your organizing document.** Submit your original and amended organizing documents (showing state filing certification if you are a corporation or an LLC) with your application.

1 Section 501(c)(3) requires that your organizing document state your exempt purpose(s), such as charitable, religious, educational, and/or scientific purposes. Check the box to confirm that your organizing document meets this requirement. Describe specifically where your organizing document meets this requirement, such as a reference to a particular article or section in your organizing document. Refer to the instructions for exempt purpose language. Location of Purpose Clause (Page, Article, and Paragraph): **Article 2** ☑

2a Section 501(c)(3) requires that upon dissolution of your organization, your remaining assets must be used exclusively for exempt purposes, such as charitable, religious, educational, and/or scientific purposes. Check the box on line 2a to confirm that your organizing document meets this requirement by express provision for the distribution of assets upon dissolution. If you rely on state law for your dissolution provision, do not check the box on line 2a and go to line 2c. ☑

2b If you checked the box on line 2a, specify the location of your dissolution clause (Page, Article, and Paragraph). Do not complete line 2c if you checked box 2a. **Article 7**

2c See the instructions for information about the operation of state law in your particular state. Check this box if you rely on operation of state law for your dissolution provision and indicate the state: ☐

Part IV Narrative Description of Your Activities

Using an attachment, describe your *past, present,* and *planned* activities in a narrative. If you believe that you have already provided some of this information in response to other parts of this application, you may summarize that information here and refer to the specific parts of the application for supporting details. You may also attach representative copies of newsletters, brochures, or similar documents for supporting details to this narrative. Remember that if this application is approved, it will be open for public inspection. Therefore, your narrative description of activities should be thorough and accurate. Refer to the instructions for information that must be included in your description.

Part V Compensation and Other Financial Arrangements With Your Officers, Directors, Trustees, Employees, and Independent Contractors

1a List the names, titles, and mailing addresses of all of your officers, directors, and trustees. For each person listed, state their total annual **compensation**, or proposed compensation, for all services to the organization, whether as an officer, employee, or other position. Use actual figures, if available. Enter "none" if no compensation is or will be paid. If additional space is needed, attach a separate sheet. Refer to the instructions for information on what to include as compensation.

Name	Title	Mailing address	Compensation amount (annual actual or estimated)
	CEO	135 Auburn Ave. Atlanta, GA 30303	NONE
	CFO		NONE
	Sectary		NONE
			NONE

Part V   Compensation and Other Financial Arrangements With Your Officers, Directors, Trustees, Employees, and Independent Contractors (Continued)

b List the names, titles, and mailing addresses of each of your five highest compensated employees who receive or will receive compensation of more than $50,000 per year. Use the actual figure, if available. Refer to the instructions for information on what to include as compensation. Do not include officers, directors, or trustees listed in line 1a.

Name	Title	Mailing address	Compensation amount (annual actual or estimated)
NA			

c List the names, names of businesses, and mailing addresses of your five highest compensated **independent contractors** that receive or will receive compensation of more than $50,000 per year. Use the actual figure, if available. Refer to the instructions for information on what to include as compensation.

Name	Title	Mailing address	Compensation amount (annual actual or estimated)
NA			

The following "Yes" or "No" questions relate to *past, present, or planned* relationships, transactions, or agreements with your officers, directors, trustees, highest compensated employees, and highest compensated independent contractors listed in lines 1a, 1b, and 1c.

2a Are any of your officers, directors, or trustees **related** to each other through **family or business relationships**? If "Yes," identify the individuals and explain the relationship. ☐ Yes ☑ No

b Do you have a business relationship with any of your officers, directors, or trustees other than through their position as an officer, director, or trustee? If "Yes," identify the individuals and describe the business relationship with each of your officers, directors, or trustees. ☐ Yes ☑ No

c Are any of your officers, directors, or trustees related to your highest compensated employees or highest compensated independent contractors listed on lines 1b or 1c through family or business relationships? If "Yes," identify the individuals and explain the relationship. ☐ Yes ☑ No

3a For each of your officers, directors, trustees, highest compensated employees, and highest compensated independent contractors listed on lines 1a, 1b, or 1c, attach a list showing their name, qualifications, average hours worked, and duties.

b Do any of your officers, directors, trustees, highest compensated employees, and highest compensated independent contractors listed on lines 1a, 1b, or 1c receive compensation from any other organizations, whether tax exempt or taxable, that are related to you through **common control**? If "Yes," identify the individuals, explain the relationship between you and the other organization, and describe the compensation arrangement. ☐ Yes ☑ No

4 In establishing the compensation for your officers, directors, trustees, highest compensated employees, and highest compensated independent contractors listed on lines 1a, 1b, and 1c, the following practices are recommended, although they are not required to obtain exemption. Answer "Yes" to all the practices you use.

a Do you or will the individuals that approve compensation arrangements follow a conflict of interest policy? ☑ Yes ☐ No

b Do you or will you approve compensation arrangements in advance of paying compensation? ☑ Yes ☐ No

c Do you or will you document in writing the date and terms of approved compensation arrangements? ☑ Yes ☐ No

28

Part V   Compensation and Other Financial Arrangements With Your Officers, Directors, Trustees, Employees, and Independent Contractors (Continued)

d	Do you or will you record in writing the decision made by each individual who decided or voted on compensation arrangements?	☑ Yes	☐ No
e	Do you or will you approve compensation arrangements based on information about compensation paid by **similarly situated** taxable or tax-exempt organizations for similar services, current compensation surveys compiled by independent firms, or actual written offers from similarly situated organizations? Refer to the instructions for Part V, lines 1a, 1b, and 1c, for information on what to include as compensation.	☑ Yes	☐ No
f	Do you or will you record in writing both the information on which you relied to base your decision and its source?	☑ Yes	☐ No
g	If you answered "No" to any item on lines 4a through 4f, describe how you set compensation that is **reasonable** for your officers, directors, trustees, highest compensated employees, and highest compensated independent contractors listed in Part V, lines 1a, 1b, and 1c.		
5a	Have you adopted a **conflict of interest policy** consistent with the sample conflict of interest policy in Appendix A to the instructions? If "Yes," provide a copy of the policy and explain how the policy has been adopted, such as by resolution of your governing board. If "No," answer lines 5b and 5c.	☑ Yes	☐ No
b	What procedures will you follow to assure that persons who have a conflict of interest will not have influence over you for setting their own compensation?		
c	What procedures will you follow to assure that persons who have a conflict of interest will not have influence over you regarding business deals with themselves?		
	Note: A conflict of interest policy is recommended though it is not required to obtain exemption. Hospitals, see Schedule C, Section I, line 14.		
6a	Do you or will you compensate any of your officers, directors, trustees, highest compensated employees, and highest compensated independent contractors listed in lines 1a, 1b, or 1c through **non-fixed payments**, such as discretionary bonuses or revenue-based payments? If "Yes," describe all non-fixed compensation arrangements, including how the amounts are determined, who is eligible for such arrangements, whether you place a limitation on total compensation, and how you determine or will determine that you pay no more than reasonable compensation for services. Refer to the instructions for Part V, lines 1a, 1b, and 1c, for information on what to include as compensation.	☐ Yes	☑ No
b	Do you or will you compensate any of your employees, other than your officers, directors, trustees, or your five highest compensated employees who receive or will receive compensation of more than $50,000 per year, through non-fixed payments, such as discretionary bonuses or revenue-based payments? If "Yes," describe all non-fixed compensation arrangements, including how the amounts are or will be determined, who is or will be eligible for such arrangements, whether you place or will place a limitation on total compensation, and how you determine or will determine that you pay no more than reasonable compensation for services. Refer to the instructions for Part V, lines 1a, 1b, and 1c, for information on what to include as compensation.	☐ Yes	☑ No
7a	Do you or will you purchase any goods, services, or assets from any of your officers, directors, trustees, highest compensated employees, or highest compensated independent contractors listed in lines 1a, 1b, or 1c? If "Yes," describe any such purchase that you made or intend to make, from whom you make or will make such purchases, how the terms are or will be negotiated at **arm's length**, and explain how you determine or will determine that you pay no more than **fair market value**. Attach copies of any written contracts or other agreements relating to such purchases.	☐ Yes	☑ No
b	Do you or will you sell any goods, services, or assets to any of your officers, directors, trustees, highest compensated employees, or highest compensated independent contractors listed in lines 1a, 1b, or 1c? If "Yes," describe any such sales that you made or intend to make, to whom you make or will make such sales, how the terms are or will be negotiated at arm's length, and explain how you determine or will determine you are or will be paid at least fair market value. Attach copies of any written contracts or other agreements relating to such sales.	☐ Yes	☑ No
8a	Do you or will you have any leases, contracts, loans, or other agreements with your officers, directors, trustees, highest compensated employees, or highest compensated independent contractors listed in lines 1a, 1b, or 1c? If "Yes," provide the information requested in lines 8b through 8f.	☐ Yes	☑ No
b	Describe any written or oral arrangements that you made or intend to make.		
c	Identify with whom you have or will have such arrangements.		
d	Explain how the terms are or will be negotiated at arm's length.		
e	Explain how you determine you pay no more than fair market value or you are paid at least fair market value.		
f	Attach copies of any signed leases, contracts, loans, or other agreements relating to such arrangements.		
9a	Do you or will you have any leases, contracts, loans, or other agreements with any organization in which any of your officers, directors, or trustees are also officers, directors, or trustees, or in which any individual officer, director, or trustee owns more than a 35% interest? If "Yes," provide the information requested in lines 9b through 9f.	☐ Yes	☑ No

29

Part V Compensation and Other Financial Arrangements With Your Officers, Directors, Trustees, Employees, and Independent Contractors (Continued)

b Describe any written or oral arrangements you made or intend to make.

c Identify with whom you have or will have such arrangements.

d Explain how the terms are or will be negotiated at arm's length.

e Explain how you determine or will determine you pay no more than fair market value or that you are paid at least fair market value.

f Attach a copy of any signed leases, contracts, loans, or other agreements relating to such arrangements.

Part VI Your Members and Other Individuals and Organizations That Receive Benefits From You

The following "Yes" or "No" questions relate to goods, services, and funds you provide to individuals and organizations as part of your activities. Your answers should pertain to past, present, and planned activities. (See instructions.)

1a	In carrying out your exempt purposes, do you provide goods, services, or funds to individuals? If "Yes," describe each program that provides goods, services, or funds to individuals.	☑ Yes	☐ No
b	In carrying out your exempt purposes, do you provide goods, services, or funds to organizations? If "Yes," describe each program that provides goods, services, or funds to organizations.	☑ Yes	☐ No
2	Do any of your programs limit the provision of goods, services, or funds to a specific individual or group of specific individuals? For example, answer "Yes," if goods, services, or funds are provided only for a particular individual, your members, individuals who work for a particular employer, or graduates of a particular school. If "Yes," explain the limitation and how recipients are selected for each program.	☐ Yes	☑ No
3	Do any individuals who receive goods, services, or funds through your programs have a family or business relationship with any officer, director, trustee, or with any of your highest compensated employees or highest compensated independent contractors listed in Part V, lines 1a, 1b, and 1c? If "Yes," explain how these related individuals are eligible for goods, services, or funds.	☐ Yes	☑ No

Part VII Your History

The following "Yes" or "No" questions relate to your history. (See instructions.)

1	Are you a successor to another organization? Answer "Yes," if you have taken or will take over the activities of another organization; you took over 25% or more of the fair market value of the net assets of another organization; or you were established upon the conversion of an organization from for-profit to non-profit status. If "Yes," complete Schedule G.	☐ Yes	☑ No
2	Are you submitting this application more than 27 months after the end of the month in which you were legally formed? If "Yes," complete Schedule E.	☐ Yes	☑ No

Part VIII Your Specific Activities

The following "Yes" or "No" questions relate to specific activities that you may conduct. Check the appropriate box. Your answers should pertain to past, present, and planned activities. (See instructions.)

1	Do you support or oppose candidates in political campaigns in any way? If "Yes," explain.	☐ Yes	☑ No
2a	Do you attempt to influence legislation? If "Yes," explain how you attempt to influence legislation and complete line 2b. If "No," go to line 3a.	☐ Yes	☑ No
b	Have you made or are you making an election to have your legislative activities measured by expenditures by filing Form 5768? If "Yes," attach a copy of the Form 5768 that was already filed or attach a completed Form 5768 that you are filing with this application. If "No," describe whether your attempts to influence legislation are a substantial part of your activities. Include the time and money spent on your attempts to influence legislation as compared to your total activities.	☐ Yes	☑ No
3a	Do you or will you operate bingo or gaming activities? If "Yes," describe who conducts them, and list all revenue received or expected to be received and expenses paid or expected to be paid in operating these activities. Revenue and expenses should be provided for the time periods specified in Part IX, Financial Data.	☐ Yes	☑ No
b	Do you or will you enter into contracts or other agreements with individuals or organizations to conduct bingo or gaming for you? If "Yes," describe any written or oral arrangements that you made or intend to make, identify with whom you have or will have such arrangements, explain how the terms are or will be negotiated at arm's length, and explain how you determine or will determine you pay no more than fair market value or you will be paid at least fair market value. Attach copies of any written contracts or other agreements relating to such arrangements.	☐ Yes	☑ No
c	List the states and local jurisdictions, including Indian Reservations, in which you conduct or will conduct gaming or bingo.		

Part VIII   Your Specific Activities *(Continued)*

4a Do you or will you undertake **fundraising**? If "Yes," check all the fundraising programs you do or will conduct. (See instructions.)   ☑ Yes   ☐ No

☑ mail solicitations   ☐ phone solicitations
☑ email solicitations   ☑ accept donations on your website
☑ personal solicitations   ☐ receive donations from another organization's website
☐ vehicle, boat, plane, or similar donations   ☑ government grant solicitations
☑ foundation grant solicitations   ☐ Other

Attach a description of each fundraising program.

b Do you or will you have written or oral contracts with any individuals or organizations to raise funds for you? If "Yes," describe these activities. Include all revenue and expenses from these activities and state who conducts them. Revenue and expenses should be provided for the time periods specified in Part IX, Financial Data. Also, attach a copy of any contracts or agreements.   ☐ Yes   ☑ No

c Do you or will you engage in fundraising activities for other organizations? If "Yes," describe these arrangements. Include a description of the organizations for which you raise funds and attach copies of all contracts or agreements.   ☐ Yes   ☑ No

d List all states and local jurisdictions in which you conduct fundraising. For each state or local jurisdiction listed, specify whether you fundraise for your own organization, you fundraise for another organization, or another organization fundraises for you.

e Do you or will you maintain separate accounts for any contributor under which the contributor has the right to advise on the use or distribution of funds? Answer "Yes" if the donor may provide advice on the types of investments, distributions from the types of investments, or the distribution from the donor's contribution account. If "Yes," describe this program, including the type of advice that may be provided and submit copies of any written materials provided to donors.   ☐ Yes   ☑ No

5 Are you **affiliated** with a governmental unit? If "Yes," explain.   ☐ Yes   ☑ No

6a Do you or will you engage in **economic development**? If "Yes," describe your program.   ☐ Yes   ☑ No
b Describe in full who benefits from your economic development activities and how the activities promote exempt purposes.

7a Do or will persons other than your employees or volunteers **develop** your facilities? If "Yes," describe each facility, the role of the developer, and any business or family relationship(s) between the developer and your officers, directors, or trustees.   ☐ Yes   ☑ No

b Do or will persons other than your employees or volunteers **manage** your activities or facilities? If "Yes," describe each activity and facility, the role of the manager, and any business or family relationship(s) between the manager and your officers, directors, or trustees.   ☐ Yes   ☑ No

c If there is a business or family relationship between any manager or developer and your officers, directors, or trustees, identify the individuals, explain the relationship, describe how contracts are negotiated at arm's length so that you pay no more than fair market value, and submit a copy of any contracts or other agreements.

8 Do you or will you enter into **joint ventures**, including partnerships or **limited liability companies** treated as partnerships, in which you share profits and losses with partners other than section 501(c)(3) organizations? If "Yes," describe the activities of those joint ventures in which you participate.   ☐ Yes   ☑ No

9a Are you applying for exemption as a childcare organization under section 501(k)? If "Yes," answer lines 9b through 9d. If "No," go to line 10.   ☐ Yes   ☑ No

b Do you provide child care so that parents or caretakers of children you care for can be **gainfully employed** (see instructions)? If "No," explain how you qualify as a childcare organization described in section 501(k).   ☐ Yes   ☑ No

c Of the children for whom you provide child care, are 85% or more of them cared for by you to enable their parents or caretakers to be gainfully employed (see instructions)? If "No," explain how you qualify as a childcare organization described in section 501(k).   ☐ Yes   ☑ No

d Are your services available to the general public? If "No," describe the specific group of people for whom your activities are available. Also, see the instructions and explain how you qualify as a childcare organization described in section 501(k).   ☑ Yes   ☐ No

10 Do you or will you publish, own, or have rights in music, literature, tapes, artworks, choreography, scientific discoveries, or other **intellectual property**? If "Yes," explain. Describe who owns or will own any copyrights, patents, or trademarks, whether fees are or will be charged, how the fees are determined, and how any items are or will be produced, distributed, and marketed   ☑ Yes   ☐ No

Part VIII   Your Specific Activities *(Continued)*

11	Do you or will you accept contributions of: real property; conservation easements; closely held securities; intellectual property such as patents, trademarks, and copyrights; works of music or art; licenses; royalties; automobiles, boats, planes, or other vehicles; or collectibles of any type? If "Yes," describe each type of contribution, any conditions imposed by the donor on the contribution, and any agreements with the donor regarding the contribution.	☑ Yes	☐ No

12a	Do you or will you operate in a **foreign country** or countries? If "Yes," answer lines 12b through 12d. If "No," go to line 13a.	☐ Yes	☑ No
b	Name the foreign countries and regions within the countries in which you operate.		
c	Describe your operations in each country and region in which you operate.		
d	Describe how your operations in each country and region further your exempt purposes.		

13a	Do you or will you make grants, loans, or other distributions to organization(s)? If "Yes," answer lines 13b through 13g. If "No," go to line 14a.	☐ Yes	☑ No
b	Describe how your grants, loans, or other distributions to organizations further your exempt purposes.		
c	Do you have written contracts with each of these organizations? If "Yes," attach a copy of each contract.	☐ Yes	☐ No
d	Identify each recipient organization and any **relationship** between you and the recipient organization.		
e	Describe the records you keep with respect to the grants, loans, or other distributions you make.		
f	Describe your selection process, including whether you do any of the following:		
	(i) Do you require an application form? If "Yes," attach a copy of the form.	☐ Yes	☐ No
	(ii) Do you require a grant proposal? If "Yes," describe whether the grant proposal specifies your responsibilities and those of the grantee, obligates the grantee to use the grant funds only for the purposes for which the grant was made, provides for periodic written reports concerning the use of grant funds, requires a final written report and an accounting of how grant funds were used, and acknowledges your authority to withhold and/or recover grant funds in case such funds are, or appear to be, misused.	☐ Yes	☐ No
g	Describe your procedures for oversight of distributions that assure you the resources are used to further your exempt purposes, including whether you require periodic and final reports on the use of resources.		

14a	Do you or will you make grants, loans, or other distributions to foreign organizations? If "Yes," answer lines 14b through 14f. If "No," go to line 15.	☐ Yes	☑ No
b	Provide the name of each foreign organization, the country and regions within a country in which each foreign organization operates, and describe any relationship you have with each foreign organization.		
c	Does any foreign organization listed in line 14b accept contributions earmarked for a specific country or specific organization? If "Yes," list all earmarked organizations or countries.	☐ Yes	☐ No
d	Do your contributors know that you have ultimate authority to use contributions made to you at your discretion for purposes consistent with your exempt purposes? If "Yes," describe how you relay this information to contributors.	☐ Yes	☐ No
e	Do you or will you make pre-grant inquiries about the recipient organization? If "Yes," describe these inquiries, including whether you inquire about the recipient's financial status, its tax-exempt status under the Internal Revenue Code, its ability to accomplish the purpose for which the resources are provided, and other relevant information.	☐ Yes	☐ No
f	Do you or will you use any additional procedures to ensure that your distributions to foreign organizations are used in furtherance of your exempt purposes? If "Yes," describe these procedures, including site visits by your employees or compliance checks by impartial experts, to verify that grant funds are being used appropriately.	☐ Yes	☐ No

Part VIII   **Your Specific Activities** *(Continued)*

		Yes	No
15	Do you have a **close connection** with any organizations? If "Yes," explain.	☐ Yes	☑ No
16	Are you applying for exemption as a **cooperative hospital service organization** under section 501(e)? If "Yes," explain.	☐ Yes	☑ No
17	Are you applying for exemption as a **cooperative service organization of operating educational organizations** under section 501(f)? If "Yes," explain.	☐ Yes	☑ No
18	Are you applying for exemption as a **charitable risk pool** under section 501(n)? If "Yes," explain.	☐ Yes	☑ No
19	Do you or will you operate a **school**? If "Yes," complete Schedule B. Answer "Yes," whether you operate a school as your main function or as a secondary activity.	☐ Yes	☑ No
20	Is your main function to provide **hospital** or **medical care**? If "Yes," complete Schedule C.	☐ Yes	☑ No
21	Do you or will you provide **low-income** housing or housing for the **elderly** or **handicapped**? If "Yes," complete Schedule F.	☐ Yes	☑ No
22	Do you or will you provide scholarships, fellowships, educational loans, or other educational grants to individuals, including grants for travel, study, or other similar purposes? If "Yes," complete Schedule H.	☐ Yes	☑ No

Note: **Private foundations** may use Schedule H to request advance approval of individual grant procedures.

33

Part IX Financial Data

For purposes of this schedule, years in existence refer to completed tax years. If in existence 4 or more years, complete the schedule for the most recent 4 tax years. If in existence more than 1 year but less than 4 years, complete the statements for each year in existence and provide projections of your likely revenues and expenses based on a reasonable and good faith estimate of your future finances for a total of 3 years of financial information. If in existence less than 1 year, provide projections of your likely revenues and expenses for the current year and the 2 following years, based on a reasonable and good faith estimate of your future finances for a total of 3 years of financial information. (See instructions.)

A. Statement of Revenues and Expenses

	Type of revenue or expense	Current tax year (a) From 5/1/06 To 12/31/06	(b) From 1/1/07 To 12/31/07	(c) From 1/1/08 To 12/31/08	(d) From ___ To ___	(e) Provide Total for (a) through (d)
Revenues	1 Gifts, grants, and contributions received (do not include unusual grants)	3,000	5,000	8,000		16,000
	2 Membership fees received					0
	3 Gross investment income					0
	4 Net unrelated business income					0
	5 Taxes levied for your benefit					0
	6 Value of services or facilities furnished by a governmental unit without charge (not including the value of services generally furnished to the public without charge)					0
	7 Any revenue not otherwise listed above or in lines 9–12 below (attach an itemized list)					0
	8 Total of lines 1 through 7	3,000	5,000	8,000		16,000
	9 Gross receipts from admissions, merchandise sold or services performed, or furnishing of facilities in any activity that is related to your exempt purposes (attach itemized list)					0
	10 Total of lines 8 and 9	3,000	5,000	8,000		16,000
	11 Net gain or loss on sale of capital assets (attach schedule and see instructions)					0
	12 Unusual grants					0
	13 Total Revenue Add lines 10 through 12	3,000	5,000	8,000		16,000
Expenses	14 Fundraising expenses					
	15 Contributions, gifts, grants, and similar amounts paid out (attach an itemized list)					
	16 Disbursements to or for the benefit of members (attach an itemized list)					
	17 Compensation of officers, directors, and trustees					
	18 Other salaries and wages					
	19 Interest expense					
	20 Occupancy (rent, utilities, etc.)					
	21 Depreciation and depletion					
	22 Professional fees					
	23 Any expense not otherwise classified, such as program services (attach itemized list)	3,000	5,000	8,000		
	24 Total Expenses Add lines 14 through 23	3,000	5,000	8,000		

Part IX Financial Data
Line 23 Detail

Expenses not otherwise classified

Expenses not otherwise classified	Current Tax Yr (a) 5/1/06 to 12/31/06	Tax Yr. (b) 1/1/07 to 12/31/07	Tax Yr (c) 1/1/08 to 12/31/08
Design/Printing of educational materials	1,000	3,000	3,000
Production of AV educational materials	2,000	2,000	5,000
Total Expenses Not Otherwise Classified	**3,000**	**5,000**	**8,000**

Part IX   Financial Data *(Continued)*

B. Balance Sheet (for your most recently completed tax year)

Year End:

			(Whole dollars)
	Assets	1	500
1	Cash	1	500
2	Accounts receivable, net	2	
3	Inventories	3	
4	Bonds and notes receivable (attach an itemized list)	4	
5	Corporate stocks (attach an itemized list)	5	
6	Loans receivable (attach an itemized list)	6	
7	Other investments (attach an itemized list)	7	
8	Depreciable and depletable assets (attach an itemized list)	8	
9	Land	9	
10	Other assets (attach an itemized list)	10	
11	Total Assets (add lines 1 through 10)	11	500
	Liabilities		
12	Accounts payable	12	
13	Contributions, gifts, grants, etc. payable	13	
14	Mortgages and notes payable (attach an itemized list)	14	
15	Other liabilities (attach an itemized list)	15	
16	Total Liabilities (add lines 12 through 15)	16	0
	Fund Balances or Net Assets		
17	Total fund balances or net assets	17	500
18	Total Liabilities and Fund Balances or Net Assets (add lines 16 and 17)	18	500

19 Have there been any substantial changes in your assets or liabilities since the end of the period shown above? If "Yes," explain.   ☐ Yes   ☑ No

Part X   Public Charity Status

Part X is designed to classify you as an organization that is either a **private foundation** or a **public charity**. Public charity status is a more favorable tax status than private foundation status. If you are a private foundation, Part X is designed to further determine whether you are a **private operating foundation**. (See instructions.)

1a Are you a private foundation? If "Yes," go to line 1b. If "No," go to line 5 and proceed as instructed. If you are unsure, see the instructions.   ☐ Yes   ☑ No

b As a private foundation, section 508(e) requires special provisions in your organizing document in addition to those that apply to all organizations described in section 501(c)(3). Check the box to confirm that your organizing document meets this requirement, whether by express provision or by reliance on operation of state law. Attach a statement that describes specifically where your organizing document meets this requirement, such as a reference to a particular article or section in your organizing document or by operation of state law. See the instructions, including Appendix B, for information about the special provisions that need to be contained in your organizing document. Go to line 2.   ☐

2 Are you a private operating foundation? To be a private operating foundation you must engage directly in the active conduct of charitable, religious, educational, and similar activities, as opposed to indirectly carrying out these activities by providing grants to individuals or other organizations. If "Yes," go to line 3. If "No," go to the signature section of Part XI.   ☐ Yes   ☑ No

3 Have you existed for one or more years? If "Yes," attach financial information showing that you are a private operating foundation; go to the signature section of Part XI. If "No," continue to line 4.   ☐ Yes   ☑ No

4 Have you attached either (1) an affidavit or opinion of counsel, (including a written affidavit or opinion from a certified public accountant or accounting firm with expertise regarding this tax law matter), that sets forth facts concerning your operations and support to demonstrate that you are likely to satisfy the requirements to be classified as a private operating foundation; or (2) a statement describing your proposed operations as a private operating foundation?   ☐ Yes   ☐ No

5 If you answered "No" to line 1a, indicate the type of public charity status you are requesting by checking one of the choices below. You may check only one box.

The organization is not a private foundation because it is:

a 509(a)(1) and 170(b)(1)(A)(i)—a church or a convention or association of churches. Complete and attach Schedule A.   ☐

b 509(a)(1) and 170(b)(1)(A)(ii)—a **school**. Complete and attach Schedule B.   ☐

c 509(a)(1) and 170(b)(1)(A)(iii)—a **hospital**, a cooperative hospital service organization, or a medical research organization operated in conjunction with a hospital. Complete and attach Schedule C.   ☐

d 509(a)(3)—an organization supporting either one or more organizations described in line 5a through c, f, g, or h or a publicly supported section 501(c)(4), (5), or (6) organization. Complete and attach Schedule D.   ☐

Part X   Public Charity Status *(Continued)*

e   509(a)(4)—an organization organized and operated exclusively for testing for public safety.   ☐

f   509(a)(1) and 170(b)(1)(A)(iv)—an organization operated for the benefit of a college or university that is owned or operated by a governmental unit.   ☐

g   509(a)(1) and 170(b)(1)(A)(vi)—an organization that receives a substantial part of its financial support in the form of contributions from publicly supported organizations, from a governmental unit, or from the general public.   ☐

h   509(a)(2)—an organization that normally receives not more than one-third of its financial support from gross **investment income** and receives more than one-third of its financial support from contributions, membership fees, and gross receipts from activities related to its exempt functions (subject to certain exceptions).   ☐

i   A publicly supported organization, but unsure if it is described in 5g or 5h. The organization would like the IRS to decide the correct status.   ☑

6   If you checked box g, h, or i in question 5 above, you must request either an **advance** or a **definitive ruling** by selecting one of the boxes below. Refer to the instructions to determine which type of ruling you are eligible to receive.

a   **Request for Advance Ruling:** By checking this box and signing the consent, pursuant to section 6501(c)(4) of the Code you request an advance ruling and agree to extend the statute of limitations on the assessment of excise tax under section 4940 of the Code. The tax will apply only if you do not establish public support status at the end of the 5-year advance ruling period. The assessment period will be extended for the 5 advance ruling years to 8 years, 4 months, and 15 days beyond the end of the first year. You have the right to refuse or limit the extension to a mutually agreed-upon period of time or issue(s). Publication 1035, *Extending the Tax Assessment Period*, provides a more detailed explanation of your rights and the consequences of the choices you make. You may obtain Publication 1035 free of charge from the IRS web site at *www.irs.gov* or by calling toll-free 1-800-829-3676. Signing this consent will not deprive you of any appeal rights to which you would otherwise be entitled. If you decide not to extend the statute of limitations, you are not eligible for an advance ruling.   ☑

Consent Fixing Period of Limitations Upon Assessment of Tax Under Section 4940 of the Internal Revenue Code

For Organization

		8/17/06
(Signature of Officer, Director, Trustee, or other authorized official)	(Type or print name of signer)	(Date)
	(Type or print title or authority of signer)	

For IRS Use Only

IRS Director, Exempt Organizations	(Date)

---

b   **Request for Definitive Ruling:** Check this box if you have completed one tax year of at least 8 full months and you are requesting a definitive ruling. To confirm your public support status, answer line 6b(i) if you checked box g in line 5 above. Answer line 6b(ii) if you checked box h in line 5 above. If you checked box i in line 5 above, answer both lines 6b(i) and (ii).   ☐

(i)   (a) Enter 2% of line 8, column (e) on Part IX-A. Statement of Revenues and Expenses.   _____

(b) Attach a list showing the name and amount contributed by each person, company, or organization whose gifts totaled more than the 2% amount. If the answer is "None," check this box.   ☐

(ii)   (a) For each year amounts are included on lines 1, 2, and 9 of Part IX-A. Statement of Revenues and Expenses, attach a list showing the name of and amount received from each **disqualified person.** If the answer is "None," check this box.   ☐

(b) For each year amounts are included on line 9 of Part IX-A. Statement of Revenues and Expenses, attach a list showing the name of and amount received from each payer, other than a disqualified person, whose payments were more than the larger of (1) 1% of line 10, Part IX-A. Statement of Revenues and Expenses, or (2) $5,000. If the answer is "None," check this box.   ☐

7   Did you receive any unusual grants during any of the years shown on Part IX-A. Statement of Revenues and Expenses? If "Yes," attach a list including the name of the contributor, the date and amount of the grant, a brief description of the grant, and explain why it is unusual.   ☐ Yes   ☑ No

Marrow For Life, Inc.   20-4705699
Application for 501 c 3
Part IV
Narrative Description of Activities

Marrow For Life, Inc. is engaged in providing educational programs and creating public awareness campaigns to enlist individuals to register with the National Marrow Donor Program as potential marrow donors. While the organization is not an affiliate of NMDP it has worked closely with its donor recruitment Specialists in assisting with donor drives.

The organization helps identify and facilitate places to hold donor drives. It assists in the recruitment and training of volunteers and provides assistance in developing public relations materials and publicity to support donor drives.

Marrow For Life has developed a web site to promote donor drives and to increase public awareness about leukemia and ways individuals can become marrow donors. The web address is www.marrowforlife.org.

Future activities include assisting patients with leukemia or other life threatening blood diseases in identifying existing programs and services to help met their needs.

Part VI
Benefits to Others

1a - Marrow For Life does not currently provide goods or funds to individuals. Future plans may include financial support to individuals as funds are available, to assist with medical care or basic needs. However, this is not a primary objective or purpose of the organization.
1b – Marrow for Life will from time to time, provide services to organizations such as the national Marrow Donor Program. Such services may include design of materials and publicity. s

Part VIII
Activities

4a - Marrow For Life will seek funding from individuals, corporations, foundations and faith based organizations to carry out its mission. Proposals will be written to seek funding for specific public relations campaigns or for general operating expenses. No fund raising has been conducted to date.

10 - It is anticipated that the organization will produce certain materials and video presentations that will be copyrighted. The organization will own the copyright but does not plan to profit from the copyrighted material. Plans are to make such material available to the general public without charge as a public service to promote awareness about leukemia and other blood disorders. Distribution of materials will be through the web site. Only costs for shipping and handling will be charged.

11 – Marrow for Life will accept contributions of real property, automobiles and other valuable assets. There are no such plans presently to solicit such gifts. Any donor imposed conditions must comply with generally accepted rules governing non profit organizations.

It is important to keep in mind that changes can occur in the application process at any time. Check to make sure you have the most recent information and the latest application forms.

Selecting the Right Board of Directors

Assembling the right board can be a challenge. People agree to serve on boards of emerging nonprofits for a variety of reasons. Sometime it is to help the nonprofit because they believe in the cause or the person who is putting it together. Unfortunately, there are times when there are other agendas. This step takes great skill, discernment and research. Make sure that each member serving on the board is very clear of what is expected and that they are willing and able to meet the challenge.

Accounting and Accountability

It is very important, especially for start-ups, that you establish guidelines for accounting. If you are not familiar with accepted accounting procedures for nonprofits, get professional help. If you set your bookkeeping process up correctly and is user- friendly software you will avoid challenges later. My personal preference is QuickBooks.

For many small nonprofits there is a tendency to mingle personal and organizational funds. This is a definite set up for disaster. Establish a separate banking account and be sure not to use the funds for personal use. If you spend your personal funds for the organization always get a receipt that includes the name of the establishment, date of purchase and amount. If you are purchasing items from the same source for business and personal use, always make it separate transactions. This separation is necessary and will help avoid challenges in the future.

It is highly recommended that you have an annual audit from an independent source. This may be an added expense but necessary. You may seek the services of a student intern to help with this process.

Compliance

Laws governing nonprofits vary by state. Check with your state to make sure you are in compliance. In Georgia after you have formed a nonprofit you are required to also file with the Secretary of State form C-100 in order to solicit funds. This form is available online at www.georgiasecretaryofstate.gov Under the Securities section you will see this form. There is a fee of $35.00, which may change and currently is renewal every two years.

Nonprofit Resources

There are a number of useful resources available for nonprofit organizations such as seminars, discounts and professional development, just to name a few. For in depth information on nonprofit board development visit: www.dorseytrainingandconsultinginc.com Also, visit http://foundationcenter.org/gainknowledge/nonprofitlinks/ for a listing of various resources available to nonprofit organizations.

Conclusion

This is the first step in developing your nonprofit organization. There are a number of web sites and publications that can provide additional information on specific subjects.

The true mission of a nonprofit should be to provide service. The 501 (c)(3) status simply allows donors to get a tax deduction for their contribution to support your work.

One way to increase your outreach is to collaborate with other nonprofits with similar missions. You should also exercise caution when using the services of fundraising organizations and individuals. Some charge exuberant fees for services and some take your money but do not produce results. It is advisable to have an attorney review all contracts and agreements and also contact sources and references to verify integrity.

There are many needs in our society. Hopefully you and your organization will make a difference. "The harvest truly is great, but the laborers are few."-Luke 10:2

NOTES